C-4550   CAREER EXAMINATION SERIES

This is your
PASSBOOK for...

Mental Health Counselor

Test Preparation Study Guide
Questions & Answers

NATIONAL LEARNING CORPORATION®

COPYRIGHT NOTICE

This book is SOLELY intended for, is sold ONLY to, and its use is RESTRICTED to individual, bona fide applicants or candidates who qualify by virtue of having seriously filed applications for appropriate license, certificate, professional and/or promotional advancement, higher school matriculation, scholarship, or other legitimate requirements of education and/or governmental authorities.

This book is NOT intended for use, class instruction, tutoring, training, duplication, copying, reprinting, excerption, or adaptation, etc., by:

1) Other publishers
2) Proprietors and/or Instructors of "Coaching" and/or Preparatory Courses
3) Personnel and/or Training Divisions of commercial, industrial, and governmental organizations
4) Schools, colleges, or universities and/or their departments and staffs, including teachers and other personnel
5) Testing Agencies or Bureaus
6) Study groups which seek by the purchase of a single volume to copy and/or duplicate and/or adapt this material for use by the group as a whole without having purchased individual volumes for each of the members of the group
7) Et al.

Such persons would be in violation of appropriate Federal and State statutes.

PROVISION OF LICENSING AGREEMENTS – Recognized educational, commercial, industrial, and governmental institutions and organizations, and others legitimately engaged in educational pursuits, including training, testing, and measurement activities, may address request for a licensing agreement to the copyright owners, who will determine whether, and under what conditions, including fees and charges, the materials in this book may be used them. In other words, a licensing facility exists for the legitimate use of the material in this book on other than an individual basis. However, it is asseverated and affirmed here that the material in this book CANNOT be used without the receipt of the express permission of such a licensing agreement from the Publishers. Inquiries re licensing should be addressed to the company, attention rights and permissions department.

All rights reserved, including the right of reproduction in whole or in part, in any form or by any means, electronic or mechanical, including photocopying, recording, or by any information storage and retrieval system, without permission in writing from the Publisher.

Copyright © 2025 by
National Learning Corporation

212 Michael Drive, Syosset, NY 11791
(516) 921-8888 • www.passbooks.com
E-mail: info@passbooks.com

PASSBOOK® SERIES

THE *PASSBOOK® SERIES* has been created to prepare applicants and candidates for the ultimate academic battlefield – the examination room.

At some time in our lives, each and every one of us may be required to take an examination – for validation, matriculation, admission, qualification, registration, certification, or licensure.

Based on the assumption that every applicant or candidate has met the basic formal educational standards, has taken the required number of courses, and read the necessary texts, the *PASSBOOK® SERIES* furnishes the one special preparation which may assure passing with confidence, instead of failing with insecurity. Examination questions – together with answers – are furnished as the basic vehicle for study so that the mysteries of the examination and its compounding difficulties may be eliminated or diminished by a sure method.

This book is meant to help you pass your examination provided that you qualify and are serious in your objective.

The entire field is reviewed through the huge store of content information which is succinctly presented through a provocative and challenging approach – the question-and-answer method.

A climate of success is established by furnishing the correct answers at the end of each test.

You soon learn to recognize types of questions, forms of questions, and patterns of questioning. You may even begin to anticipate expected outcomes.

You perceive that many questions are repeated or adapted so that you can gain acute insights, which may enable you to score many sure points.

You learn how to confront new questions, or types of questions, and to attack them confidently and work out the correct answers.

You note objectives and emphases, and recognize pitfalls and dangers, so that you may make positive educational adjustments.

Moreover, you are kept fully informed in relation to new concepts, methods, practices, and directions in the field.

You discover that you are actually taking the examination all the time: you are preparing for the examination by "taking" an examination, not by reading extraneous and/or supererogatory textbooks.

In short, this PASSBOOK®, used directedly, should be an important factor in helping you to pass your test.

MENTAL HEALTH COUNSELOR

DUTIES:
Provides professional mental health counseling services with an emphasis on prevention; performs related duties as required.

SUBJECT OF EXAMINATION:
A written test designed to evaluate knowledge, skills and /or abilities in the following areas:

1. **Characteristics and problems of individuals with mental illness** - These questions test for knowledge and understanding of the symptoms, causes, characteristics, and treatment approaches associated with mental illness.
2. **Developing & implementing treatment in a social work program** - These questions test for knowledge, understanding, and ability to apply social work concepts, theories, principles, and practices in a mental hygiene program which provides services to clients who have various mental hygiene conditions such as mental illness, developmental disabilities or addiction. Questions may cover such topics as assessment, development, and implementation of treatment; coordination of treatment; evaluation of treatment; coordination of services; social work standards; roles of treatment team members; individual, family, and group counseling; community services; behavior management; crisis intervention; and patient/client advocacy.
3. **Preparing written material** - These questions test for the ability to present information clearly and accurately, and to organize paragraphs logically and comprehensibly. For some questions, you will be given information in two or three sentences followed by four restatements of the information. You must then choose the best version. For other questions, you will be given paragraphs with their sentences out of order. You must then choose, from four suggestions, the best order for the sentences.
4. **Working with individuals to promote mental health** - These questions test for knowledge of characteristics, causes and treatment methods associated with chronic mental illness and/or addiction. Questions cover such topics as establishing, maintaining and terminating client relationships; recognizing, interpreting, and responding to individual and group behaviors; providing access to essential services such as financial, housing, medical, educational, legal, vocational, and recreational; and eligibility criteria of programs and agencies offering such services.

HOW TO TAKE A TEST

I. YOU MUST PASS AN EXAMINATION

A. *WHAT EVERY CANDIDATE SHOULD KNOW*

Examination applicants often ask us for help in preparing for the written test. What can I study in advance? What kinds of questions will be asked? How will the test be given? How will the papers be graded?

As an applicant for a civil service examination, you may be wondering about some of these things. Our purpose here is to suggest effective methods of advance study and to describe civil service examinations.

Your chances for success on this examination can be increased if you know how to prepare. Those "pre-examination jitters" can be reduced if you know what to expect. You can even experience an adventure in good citizenship if you know why civil service exams are given.

B. *WHY ARE CIVIL SERVICE EXAMINATIONS GIVEN?*

Civil service examinations are important to you in two ways. As a citizen, you want public jobs filled by employees who know how to do their work. As a job seeker, you want a fair chance to compete for that job on an equal footing with other candidates. The best-known means of accomplishing this two-fold goal is the competitive examination.

Exams are widely publicized throughout the nation. They may be administered for jobs in federal, state, city, municipal, town or village governments or agencies.

Any citizen may apply, with some limitations, such as the age or residence of applicants. Your experience and education may be reviewed to see whether you meet the requirements for the particular examination. When these requirements exist, they are reasonable and applied consistently to all applicants. Thus, a competitive examination may cause you some uneasiness now, but it is your privilege and safeguard.

C. *HOW ARE CIVIL SERVICE EXAMS DEVELOPED?*

Examinations are carefully written by trained technicians who are specialists in the field known as "psychological measurement," in consultation with recognized authorities in the field of work that the test will cover. These experts recommend the subject matter areas or skills to be tested; only those knowledges or skills important to your success on the job are included. The most reliable books and source materials available are used as references. Together, the experts and technicians judge the difficulty level of the questions.

Test technicians know how to phrase questions so that the problem is clearly stated. Their ethics do not permit "trick" or "catch" questions. Questions may have been tried out on sample groups, or subjected to statistical analysis, to determine their usefulness.

Written tests are often used in combination with performance tests, ratings of training and experience, and oral interviews. All of these measures combine to form the best-known means of finding the right person for the right job.

II. HOW TO PASS THE WRITTEN TEST

A. NATURE OF THE EXAMINATION

To prepare intelligently for civil service examinations, you should know how they differ from school examinations you have taken. In school you were assigned certain definite pages to read or subjects to cover. The examination questions were quite detailed and usually emphasized memory. Civil service exams, on the other hand, try to discover your present ability to perform the duties of a position, plus your potentiality to learn these duties. In other words, a civil service exam attempts to predict how successful you will be. Questions cover such a broad area that they cannot be as minute and detailed as school exam questions.

In the public service similar kinds of work, or positions, are grouped together in one "class." This process is known as *position-classification*. All the positions in a class are paid according to the salary range for that class. One class title covers all of these positions, and they are all tested by the same examination.

B. FOUR BASIC STEPS

1) Study the announcement

How, then, can you know what subjects to study? Our best answer is: "Learn as much as possible about the class of positions for which you've applied." The exam will test the knowledge, skills and abilities needed to do the work.

Your most valuable source of information about the position you want is the official exam announcement. This announcement lists the training and experience qualifications. Check these standards and apply only if you come reasonably close to meeting them.

The brief description of the position in the examination announcement offers some clues to the subjects which will be tested. Think about the job itself. Review the duties in your mind. Can you perform them, or are there some in which you are rusty? Fill in the blank spots in your preparation.

Many jurisdictions preview the written test in the exam announcement by including a section called "Knowledge and Abilities Required," "Scope of the Examination," or some similar heading. Here you will find out specifically what fields will be tested.

2) Review your own background

Once you learn in general what the position is all about, and what you need to know to do the work, ask yourself which subjects you already know fairly well and which need improvement. You may wonder whether to concentrate on improving your strong areas or on building some background in your fields of weakness. When the announcement has specified "some knowledge" or "considerable knowledge," or has used adjectives like "beginning principles of..." or "advanced ... methods," you can get a clue as to the number and difficulty of questions to be asked in any given field. More questions, and hence broader coverage, would be included for those subjects which are more important in the work. Now weigh your strengths and weaknesses against the job requirements and prepare accordingly.

3) Determine the level of the position

Another way to tell how intensively you should prepare is to understand the level of the job for which you are applying. Is it the entering level? In other words, is this the position in which beginners in a field of work are hired? Or is it an intermediate or advanced level? Sometimes this is indicated by such words as "Junior" or "Senior" in the class title. Other jurisdictions use Roman numerals to designate the level – Clerk I, Clerk II, for example. The word "Supervisor" sometimes appears in the title. If the level is not indicated by the title, check the description of duties. Will you be working under very close supervision, or will you have responsibility for independent decisions in this work?

4) Choose appropriate study materials

Now that you know the subjects to be examined and the relative amount of each subject to be covered, you can choose suitable study materials. For beginning level jobs, or even advanced ones, if you have a pronounced weakness in some aspect of your training, read a modern, standard textbook in that field. Be sure it is up to date and has general coverage. Such books are normally available at your library, and the librarian will be glad to help you locate one. For entry-level positions, questions of appropriate difficulty are chosen – neither highly advanced questions, nor those too simple. Such questions require careful thought but not advanced training.

If the position for which you are applying is technical or advanced, you will read more advanced, specialized material. If you are already familiar with the basic principles of your field, elementary textbooks would waste your time. Concentrate on advanced textbooks and technical periodicals. Think through the concepts and review difficult problems in your field.

These are all general sources. You can get more ideas on your own initiative, following these leads. For example, training manuals and publications of the government agency which employs workers in your field can be useful, particularly for technical and professional positions. A letter or visit to the government department involved may result in more specific study suggestions, and certainly will provide you with a more definite idea of the exact nature of the position you are seeking.

III. KINDS OF TESTS

Tests are used for purposes other than measuring knowledge and ability to perform specified duties. For some positions, it is equally important to test ability to make adjustments to new situations or to profit from training. In others, basic mental abilities not dependent on information are essential. Questions which test these things may not appear as pertinent to the duties of the position as those which test for knowledge and information. Yet they are often highly important parts of a fair examination. For very general questions, it is almost impossible to help you direct your study efforts. What we can do is to point out some of the more common of these general abilities needed in public service positions and describe some typical questions.

1) General information

Broad, general information has been found useful for predicting job success in some kinds of work. This is tested in a variety of ways, from vocabulary lists to questions about current events. Basic background in some field of work, such as sociology or economics, may be sampled in a group of questions. Often these are principles which have become familiar to most persons through exposure rather than through formal training. It is difficult to advise you how to study for these questions; being alert to the world around you is our best suggestion.

2) Verbal ability

An example of an ability needed in many positions is verbal or language ability. Verbal ability is, in brief, the ability to use and understand words. Vocabulary and grammar tests are typical measures of this ability. Reading comprehension or paragraph interpretation questions are common in many kinds of civil service tests. You are given a paragraph of written material and asked to find its central meaning.

3) Numerical ability

Number skills can be tested by the familiar arithmetic problem, by checking paired lists of numbers to see which are alike and which are different, or by interpreting charts and graphs. In the latter test, a graph may be printed in the test booklet which you are asked to use as the basis for answering questions.

4) Observation

A popular test for law-enforcement positions is the observation test. A picture is shown to you for several minutes, then taken away. Questions about the picture test your ability to observe both details and larger elements.

5) Following directions

In many positions in the public service, the employee must be able to carry out written instructions dependably and accurately. You may be given a chart with several columns, each column listing a variety of information. The questions require you to carry out directions involving the information given in the chart.

6) Skills and aptitudes

Performance tests effectively measure some manual skills and aptitudes. When the skill is one in which you are trained, such as typing or shorthand, you can practice. These tests are often very much like those given in business school or high school courses. For many of the other skills and aptitudes, however, no short-time preparation can be made. Skills and abilities natural to you or that you have developed throughout your lifetime are being tested.

Many of the general questions just described provide all the data needed to answer the questions and ask you to use your reasoning ability to find the answers. Your best preparation for these tests, as well as for tests of facts and ideas, is to be at your physical and mental best. You, no doubt, have your own methods of getting into an exam-taking mood and keeping "in shape." The next section lists some ideas on this subject.

IV. KINDS OF QUESTIONS

Only rarely is the "essay" question, which you answer in narrative form, used in civil service tests. Civil service tests are usually of the short-answer type. Full instructions for answering these questions will be given to you at the examination. But in case this is your first experience with short-answer questions and separate answer sheets, here is what you need to know:

1) **Multiple-choice Questions**

Most popular of the short-answer questions is the "multiple choice" or "best answer" question. It can be used, for example, to test for factual knowledge, ability to solve problems or judgment in meeting situations found at work.

A multiple-choice question is normally one of three types—
- It can begin with an incomplete statement followed by several possible endings. You are to find the one ending which *best* completes the statement, although some of the others may not be entirely wrong.
- It can also be a complete statement in the form of a question which is answered by choosing one of the statements listed.

- It can be in the form of a problem – again you select the best answer.

Here is an example of a multiple-choice question with a discussion which should give you some clues as to the method for choosing the right answer:

When an employee has a complaint about his assignment, the action which will *best* help him overcome his difficulty is to
  A. discuss his difficulty with his coworkers
  B. take the problem to the head of the organization
  C. take the problem to the person who gave him the assignment
  D. say nothing to anyone about his complaint

In answering this question, you should study each of the choices to find which is best. Consider choice "A" – Certainly an employee may discuss his complaint with fellow employees, but no change or improvement can result, and the complaint remains unresolved. Choice "B" is a poor choice since the head of the organization probably does not know what assignment you have been given, and taking your problem to him is known as "going over the head" of the supervisor. The supervisor, or person who made the assignment, is the person who can clarify it or correct any injustice. Choice "C" is, therefore, correct. To say nothing, as in choice "D," is unwise. Supervisors have and interest in knowing the problems employees are facing, and the employee is seeking a solution to his problem.

2) True/False Questions

The "true/false" or "right/wrong" form of question is sometimes used. Here a complete statement is given. Your job is to decide whether the statement is right or wrong.

SAMPLE: A roaming cell-phone call to a nearby city costs less than a non-roaming call to a distant city.

This statement is wrong, or false, since roaming calls are more expensive.

This is not a complete list of all possible question forms, although most of the others are variations of these common types. You will always get complete directions for answering questions. Be sure you understand *how* to mark your answers – ask questions until you do.

V. RECORDING YOUR ANSWERS

Computer terminals are used more and more today for many different kinds of exams.

For an examination with very few applicants, you may be told to record your answers in the test booklet itself. Separate answer sheets are much more common. If this separate answer sheet is to be scored by machine – and this is often the case – it is highly important that you mark your answers correctly in order to get credit.

An electronic scoring machine is often used in civil service offices because of the speed with which papers can be scored. Machine-scored answer sheets must be marked with a pencil, which will be given to you. This pencil has a high graphite content which responds to the electronic scoring machine. As a matter of fact, stray dots may register as answers, so do not let your pencil rest on the answer sheet while you are pondering the correct answer. Also, if your pencil lead breaks or is otherwise defective, ask for another.

Since the answer sheet will be dropped in a slot in the scoring machine, be careful not to bend the corners or get the paper crumpled.

The answer sheet normally has five vertical columns of numbers, with 30 numbers to a column. These numbers correspond to the question numbers in your test booklet. After each number, going across the page are four or five pairs of dotted lines. These short dotted lines have small letters or numbers above them. The first two pairs may also have a "T" or "F" above the letters. This indicates that the first two pairs only are to be used if the questions are of the true-false type. If the questions are multiple choice, disregard the "T" and "F" and pay attention only to the small letters or numbers.

Answer your questions in the manner of the sample that follows:

32. The largest city in the United States is
    A. Washington, D.C.
    B. New York City
    C. Chicago
    D. Detroit
    E. San Francisco

1) Choose the answer you think is best. (New York City is the largest, so "B" is correct.)
2) Find the row of dotted lines numbered the same as the question you are answering. (Find row number 32)
3) Find the pair of dotted lines corresponding to the answer. (Find the pair of lines under the mark "B.")
4) Make a solid black mark between the dotted lines.

VI. BEFORE THE TEST

Common sense will help you find procedures to follow to get ready for an examination. Too many of us, however, overlook these sensible measures. Indeed, nervousness and fatigue have been found to be the most serious reasons why applicants fail to do their best on civil service tests. Here is a list of reminders:

- Begin your preparation early – Don't wait until the last minute to go scurrying around for books and materials or to find out what the position is all about.
- Prepare continuously – An hour a night for a week is better than an all-night cram session. This has been definitely established. What is more, a night a week for a month will return better dividends than crowding your study into a shorter period of time.
- Locate the place of the exam – You have been sent a notice telling you when and where to report for the examination. If the location is in a different town or otherwise unfamiliar to you, it would be well to inquire the best route and learn something about the building.
- Relax the night before the test – Allow your mind to rest. Do not study at all that night. Plan some mild recreation or diversion; then go to bed early and get a good night's sleep.
- Get up early enough to make a leisurely trip to the place for the test – This way unforeseen events, traffic snarls, unfamiliar buildings, etc. will not upset you.
- Dress comfortably – A written test is not a fashion show. You will be known by number and not by name, so wear something comfortable.

- Leave excess paraphernalia at home – Shopping bags and odd bundles will get in your way. You need bring only the items mentioned in the official notice you received; usually everything you need is provided. Do not bring reference books to the exam. They will only confuse those last minutes and be taken away from you when in the test room.
- Arrive somewhat ahead of time – If because of transportation schedules you must get there very early, bring a newspaper or magazine to take your mind off yourself while waiting.
- Locate the examination room – When you have found the proper room, you will be directed to the seat or part of the room where you will sit. Sometimes you are given a sheet of instructions to read while you are waiting. Do not fill out any forms until you are told to do so; just read them and be prepared.
- Relax and prepare to listen to the instructions
- If you have any physical problem that may keep you from doing your best, be sure to tell the test administrator. If you are sick or in poor health, you really cannot do your best on the exam. You can come back and take the test some other time.

VII. AT THE TEST

The day of the test is here and you have the test booklet in your hand. The temptation to get going is very strong. Caution! There is more to success than knowing the right answers. You must know how to identify your papers and understand variations in the type of short-answer question used in this particular examination. Follow these suggestions for maximum results from your efforts:

1) Cooperate with the monitor

The test administrator has a duty to create a situation in which you can be as much at ease as possible. He will give instructions, tell you when to begin, check to see that you are marking your answer sheet correctly, and so on. He is not there to guard you, although he will see that your competitors do not take unfair advantage. He wants to help you do your best.

2) Listen to all instructions

Don't jump the gun! Wait until you understand all directions. In most civil service tests you get more time than you need to answer the questions. So don't be in a hurry. Read each word of instructions until you clearly understand the meaning. Study the examples, listen to all announcements and follow directions. Ask questions if you do not understand what to do.

3) Identify your papers

Civil service exams are usually identified by number only. You will be assigned a number; you must not put your name on your test papers. Be sure to copy your number correctly. Since more than one exam may be given, copy your exact examination title.

4) Plan your time

Unless you are told that a test is a "speed" or "rate of work" test, speed itself is usually not important. Time enough to answer all the questions will be provided, but this does not mean that you have all day. An overall time limit has been set. Divide the total time (in minutes) by the number of questions to determine the approximate time you have for each question.

5) Do not linger over difficult questions

If you come across a difficult question, mark it with a paper clip (useful to have along) and come back to it when you have been through the booklet. One caution if you do this – be sure to skip a number on your answer sheet as well. Check often to be sure that you have not lost your place and that you are marking in the row numbered the same as the question you are answering.

6) Read the questions

Be sure you know what the question asks! Many capable people are unsuccessful because they failed to *read* the questions correctly.

7) Answer all questions

Unless you have been instructed that a penalty will be deducted for incorrect answers, it is better to guess than to omit a question.

8) Speed tests

It is often better NOT to guess on speed tests. It has been found that on timed tests people are tempted to spend the last few seconds before time is called in marking answers at random – without even reading them – in the hope of picking up a few extra points. To discourage this practice, the instructions may warn you that your score will be "corrected" for guessing. That is, a penalty will be applied. The incorrect answers will be deducted from the correct ones, or some other penalty formula will be used.

9) Review your answers

If you finish before time is called, go back to the questions you guessed or omitted to give them further thought. Review other answers if you have time.

10) Return your test materials

If you are ready to leave before others have finished or time is called, take ALL your materials to the monitor and leave quietly. Never take any test material with you. The monitor can discover whose papers are not complete, and taking a test booklet may be grounds for disqualification.

VIII. EXAMINATION TECHNIQUES

1) Read the general instructions carefully. These are usually printed on the first page of the exam booklet. As a rule, these instructions refer to the timing of the examination; the fact that you should not start work until the signal and must stop work at a signal, etc. If there are any *special* instructions, such as a choice of questions to be answered, make sure that you note this instruction carefully.

2) When you are ready to start work on the examination, that is as soon as the signal has been given, read the instructions to each question booklet, underline any key words or phrases, such as *least, best, outline, describe* and the like. In this way you will tend to answer as requested rather than discover on reviewing your paper that you *listed without describing*, that you selected the *worst* choice rather than the *best* choice, etc.

3) If the examination is of the objective or multiple-choice type – that is, each question will also give a series of possible answers: A, B, C or D, and you are called upon to select the best answer and write the letter next to that answer on your answer paper – it is advisable to start answering each question in turn. There may be anywhere from 50 to 100 such questions in the three or four hours allotted and you can see how much time would be taken if you read through all the questions before beginning to answer any. Furthermore, if you come across a question or group of questions which you know would be difficult to answer, it would undoubtedly affect your handling of all the other questions.

4) If the examination is of the essay type and contains but a few questions, it is a moot point as to whether you should read all the questions before starting to answer any one. Of course, if you are given a choice – say five out of seven and the like – then it is essential to read all the questions so you can eliminate the two that are most difficult. If, however, you are asked to answer all the questions, there may be danger in trying to answer the easiest one first because you may find that you will spend too much time on it. The best technique is to answer the first question, then proceed to the second, etc.

5) Time your answers. Before the exam begins, write down the time it started, then add the time allowed for the examination and write down the time it must be completed, then divide the time available somewhat as follows:
    - If 3-1/2 hours are allowed, that would be 210 minutes. If you have 80 objective-type questions, that would be an average of 2-1/2 minutes per question. Allow yourself no more than 2 minutes per question, or a total of 160 minutes, which will permit about 50 minutes to review.
    - If for the time allotment of 210 minutes there are 7 essay questions to answer, that would average about 30 minutes a question. Give yourself only 25 minutes per question so that you have about 35 minutes to review.

6) The most important instruction is to *read each question* and make sure you know what is wanted. The second most important instruction is to *time yourself properly* so that you answer every question. The third most important instruction is to *answer every question*. Guess if you have to but include something for each question. Remember that you will receive no credit for a blank and will probably receive some credit if you write something in answer to an essay question. If you guess a letter – say "B" for a multiple-choice question – you may have guessed right. If you leave a blank as an answer to a multiple-choice question, the examiners may respect your feelings but it will not add a point to your score. Some exams may penalize you for wrong answers, so in such cases *only*, you may not want to guess unless you have some basis for your answer.

7) Suggestions
    a. Objective-type questions
        1. Examine the question booklet for proper sequence of pages and questions
        2. Read all instructions carefully
        3. Skip any question which seems too difficult; return to it after all other questions have been answered
        4. Apportion your time properly; do not spend too much time on any single question or group of questions

5. Note and underline key words – *all, most, fewest, least, best, worst, same, opposite,* etc.
6. Pay particular attention to negatives
7. Note unusual option, e.g., unduly long, short, complex, different or similar in content to the body of the question
8. Observe the use of "hedging" words – *probably, may, most likely,* etc.
9. Make sure that your answer is put next to the same number as the question
10. Do not second-guess unless you have good reason to believe the second answer is definitely more correct
11. Cross out original answer if you decide another answer is more accurate; do not erase until you are ready to hand your paper in
12. Answer all questions; guess unless instructed otherwise
13. Leave time for review

  b. Essay questions
    1. Read each question carefully
    2. Determine exactly what is wanted. Underline key words or phrases.
    3. Decide on outline or paragraph answer
    4. Include many different points and elements unless asked to develop any one or two points or elements
    5. Show impartiality by giving pros and cons unless directed to select one side only
    6. Make and write down any assumptions you find necessary to answer the questions
    7. Watch your English, grammar, punctuation and choice of words
    8. Time your answers; don't crowd material

8) Answering the essay question

Most essay questions can be answered by framing the specific response around several key words or ideas. Here are a few such key words or ideas:

M's: manpower, materials, methods, money, management
P's: purpose, program, policy, plan, procedure, practice, problems, pitfalls, personnel, public relations

  a. Six basic steps in handling problems:
    1. Preliminary plan and background development
    2. Collect information, data and facts
    3. Analyze and interpret information, data and facts
    4. Analyze and develop solutions as well as make recommendations
    5. Prepare report and sell recommendations
    6. Install recommendations and follow up effectiveness

  b. Pitfalls to avoid
    1. *Taking things for granted* – A statement of the situation does not necessarily imply that each of the elements is necessarily true; for example, a complaint may be invalid and biased so that all that can be taken for granted is that a complaint has been registered

2. *Considering only one side of a situation* – Wherever possible, indicate several alternatives and then point out the reasons you selected the best one
3. *Failing to indicate follow up* – Whenever your answer indicates action on your part, make certain that you will take proper follow-up action to see how successful your recommendations, procedures or actions turn out to be
4. *Taking too long in answering any single question* – Remember to time your answers properly

IX. AFTER THE TEST

Scoring procedures differ in detail among civil service jurisdictions although the general principles are the same. Whether the papers are hand-scored or graded by machine we have described, they are nearly always graded by number. That is, the person who marks the paper knows only the number – never the name – of the applicant. Not until all the papers have been graded will they be matched with names. If other tests, such as training and experience or oral interview ratings have been given, scores will be combined. Different parts of the examination usually have different weights. For example, the written test might count 60 percent of the final grade, and a rating of training and experience 40 percent. In many jurisdictions, veterans will have a certain number of points added to their grades.

After the final grade has been determined, the names are placed in grade order and an eligible list is established. There are various methods for resolving ties between those who get the same final grade – probably the most common is to place first the name of the person whose application was received first. Job offers are made from the eligible list in the order the names appear on it. You will be notified of your grade and your rank as soon as all these computations have been made. This will be done as rapidly as possible.

People who are found to meet the requirements in the announcement are called "eligibles." Their names are put on a list of eligible candidates. An eligible's chances of getting a job depend on how high he stands on this list and how fast agencies are filling jobs from the list.

When a job is to be filled from a list of eligibles, the agency asks for the names of people on the list of eligibles for that job. When the civil service commission receives this request, it sends to the agency the names of the three people highest on this list. Or, if the job to be filled has specialized requirements, the office sends the agency the names of the top three persons who meet these requirements from the general list.

The appointing officer makes a choice from among the three people whose names were sent to him. If the selected person accepts the appointment, the names of the others are put back on the list to be considered for future openings.

That is the rule in hiring from all kinds of eligible lists, whether they are for typist, carpenter, chemist, or something else. For every vacancy, the appointing officer has his choice of any one of the top three eligibles on the list. This explains why the person whose name is on top of the list sometimes does not get an appointment when some of the persons lower on the list do. If the appointing officer chooses the second or third eligible, the No. 1 eligible does not get a job at once, but stays on the list until he is appointed or the list is terminated.

X. HOW TO PASS THE INTERVIEW TEST

The examination for which you applied requires an oral interview test. You have already taken the written test and you are now being called for the interview test – the final part of the formal examination.

You may think that it is not possible to prepare for an interview test and that there are no procedures to follow during an interview. Our purpose is to point out some things you can do in advance that will help you and some good rules to follow and pitfalls to avoid while you are being interviewed.

What is an interview supposed to test?

The written examination is designed to test the technical knowledge and competence of the candidate; the oral is designed to evaluate intangible qualities, not readily measured otherwise, and to establish a list showing the relative fitness of each candidate – as measured against his competitors – for the position sought. Scoring is not on the basis of "right" and "wrong," but on a sliding scale of values ranging from "not passable" to "outstanding." As a matter of fact, it is possible to achieve a relatively low score without a single "incorrect" answer because of evident weakness in the qualities being measured.

Occasionally, an examination may consist entirely of an oral test – either an individual or a group oral. In such cases, information is sought concerning the technical knowledges and abilities of the candidate, since there has been no written examination for this purpose. More commonly, however, an oral test is used to supplement a written examination.

Who conducts interviews?

The composition of oral boards varies among different jurisdictions. In nearly all, a representative of the personnel department serves as chairman. One of the members of the board may be a representative of the department in which the candidate would work. In some cases, "outside experts" are used, and, frequently, a businessman or some other representative of the general public is asked to serve. Labor and management or other special groups may be represented. The aim is to secure the services of experts in the appropriate field.

However the board is composed, it is a good idea (and not at all improper or unethical) to ascertain in advance of the interview who the members are and what groups they represent. When you are introduced to them, you will have some idea of their backgrounds and interests, and at least you will not stutter and stammer over their names.

What should be done before the interview?

While knowledge about the board members is useful and takes some of the surprise element out of the interview, there is other preparation which is more substantive. It *is* possible to prepare for an oral interview – in several ways:

1) Keep a copy of your application and review it carefully before the interview

This may be the only document before the oral board, and the starting point of the interview. Know what education and experience you have listed there, and the sequence and dates of all of it. Sometimes the board will ask you to review the highlights of your experience for them; you should not have to hem and haw doing it.

2) Study the class specification and the examination announcement

Usually, the oral board has one or both of these to guide them. The qualities, characteristics or knowledges required by the position sought are stated in these documents. They offer valuable clues as to the nature of the oral interview. For example, if the job involves supervisory responsibilities, the announcement will usually indicate that knowledge of modern supervisory methods and the qualifications of the candidate as a supervisor will be tested. If so, you can expect such questions, frequently in the form of a hypothetical situation which you are expected to solve. NEVER go into an oral without knowledge of the duties and responsibilities of the job you seek.

3) Think through each qualification required

Try to visualize the kind of questions you would ask if you were a board member. How well could you answer them? Try especially to appraise your own knowledge and background in each area, *measured against the job sought*, and identify any areas in which you are weak. Be critical and realistic – do not flatter yourself.

4) Do some general reading in areas in which you feel you may be weak

For example, if the job involves supervision and your past experience has NOT, some general reading in supervisory methods and practices, particularly in the field of human relations, might be useful. Do NOT study agency procedures or detailed manuals. The oral board will be testing your understanding and capacity, not your memory.

5) Get a good night's sleep and watch your general health and mental attitude

You will want a clear head at the interview. Take care of a cold or any other minor ailment, and of course, no hangovers.

What should be done on the day of the interview?

Now comes the day of the interview itself. Give yourself plenty of time to get there. Plan to arrive somewhat ahead of the scheduled time, particularly if your appointment is in the fore part of the day. If a previous candidate fails to appear, the board might be ready for you a bit early. By early afternoon an oral board is almost invariably behind schedule if there are many candidates, and you may have to wait. Take along a book or magazine to read, or your application to review, but leave any extraneous material in the waiting room when you go in for your interview. In any event, relax and compose yourself.

The matter of dress is important. The board is forming impressions about you – from your experience, your manners, your attitude, and your appearance. Give your personal appearance careful attention. Dress your best, but not your flashiest. Choose conservative, appropriate clothing, and be sure it is immaculate. This is a business interview, and your appearance should indicate that you regard it as such. Besides, being well groomed and properly dressed will help boost your confidence.

Sooner or later, someone will call your name and escort you into the interview room. *This is it*. From here on you are on your own. It is too late for any more preparation. But remember, you asked for this opportunity to prove your fitness, and you are here because your request was granted.

What happens when you go in?

The usual sequence of events will be as follows: The clerk (who is often the board stenographer) will introduce you to the chairman of the oral board, who will introduce you to the other members of the board. Acknowledge the introductions before you sit down. Do not be surprised if you find a microphone facing you or a stenotypist sitting by. Oral interviews are usually recorded in the event of an appeal or other review.

Usually the chairman of the board will open the interview by reviewing the highlights of your education and work experience from your application – primarily for the benefit of the other members of the board, as well as to get the material into the record. Do not interrupt or comment unless there is an error or significant misinterpretation; if that is the case, do not hesitate. But do not quibble about insignificant matters. Also, he will usually ask you some question about your education, experience or your present job – partly to get you to start talking and to establish the interviewing "rapport." He may start the actual questioning, or turn it over to one of the other members. Frequently, each member undertakes the questioning on a particular area, one in which he is perhaps most competent, so you can expect each member to participate in the examination. Because time is limited, you may also expect some rather abrupt switches in the direction the questioning takes, so do not be upset by it. Normally, a board member will not pursue a single line of questioning unless he discovers a particular strength or weakness.

After each member has participated, the chairman will usually ask whether any member has any further questions, then will ask you if you have anything you wish to add. Unless you are expecting this question, it may floor you. Worse, it may start you off on an extended, extemporaneous speech. The board is not usually seeking more information. The question is principally to offer you a last opportunity to present further qualifications or to indicate that you have nothing to add. So, if you feel that a significant qualification or characteristic has been overlooked, it is proper to point it out in a sentence or so. Do not compliment the board on the thoroughness of their examination – they have been sketchy, and you know it. If you wish, merely say, "No thank you, I have nothing further to add." This is a point where you can "talk yourself out" of a good impression or fail to present an important bit of information. Remember, *you close the interview yourself.*

The chairman will then say, "That is all, Mr. _____, thank you." Do not be startled; the interview is over, and quicker than you think. Thank him, gather your belongings and take your leave. Save your sigh of relief for the other side of the door.

How to put your best foot forward
Throughout this entire process, you may feel that the board individually and collectively is trying to pierce your defenses, seek out your hidden weaknesses and embarrass and confuse you. Actually, this is not true. They are obliged to make an appraisal of your qualifications for the job you are seeking, and they want to see you in your best light. Remember, they must interview all candidates and a non-cooperative candidate may become a failure in spite of their best efforts to bring out his qualifications. Here are 15 suggestions that will help you:

1) Be natural – Keep your attitude confident, not cocky
If you are not confident that you can do the job, do not expect the board to be. Do not apologize for your weaknesses, try to bring out your strong points. The board is interested in a positive, not negative, presentation. Cockiness will antagonize any board member and make him wonder if you are covering up a weakness by a false show of strength.

2) Get comfortable, but don't lounge or sprawl
Sit erectly but not stiffly. A careless posture may lead the board to conclude that you are careless in other things, or at least that you are not impressed by the importance of the occasion. Either conclusion is natural, even if incorrect. Do not fuss with your clothing, a pencil or an ashtray. Your hands may occasionally be useful to emphasize a point; do not let them become a point of distraction.

3) Do not wisecrack or make small talk
This is a serious situation, and your attitude should show that you consider it as such. Further, the time of the board is limited – they do not want to waste it, and neither should you.

4) Do not exaggerate your experience or abilities

In the first place, from information in the application or other interviews and sources, the board may know more about you than you think. Secondly, you probably will not get away with it. An experienced board is rather adept at spotting such a situation, so do not take the chance.

5) If you know a board member, do not make a point of it, yet do not hide it

Certainly you are not fooling him, and probably not the other members of the board. Do not try to take advantage of your acquaintanceship – it will probably do you little good.

6) Do not dominate the interview

Let the board do that. They will give you the clues – do not assume that you have to do all the talking. Realize that the board has a number of questions to ask you, and do not try to take up all the interview time by showing off your extensive knowledge of the answer to the first one.

7) Be attentive

You only have 20 minutes or so, and you should keep your attention at its sharpest throughout. When a member is addressing a problem or question to you, give him your undivided attention. Address your reply principally to him, but do not exclude the other board members.

8) Do not interrupt

A board member may be stating a problem for you to analyze. He will ask you a question when the time comes. Let him state the problem, and wait for the question.

9) Make sure you understand the question

Do not try to answer until you are sure what the question is. If it is not clear, restate it in your own words or ask the board member to clarify it for you. However, do not haggle about minor elements.

10) Reply promptly but not hastily

A common entry on oral board rating sheets is "candidate responded readily," or "candidate hesitated in replies." Respond as promptly and quickly as you can, but do not jump to a hasty, ill-considered answer.

11) Do not be peremptory in your answers

A brief answer is proper – but do not fire your answer back. That is a losing game from your point of view. The board member can probably ask questions much faster than you can answer them.

12) Do not try to create the answer you think the board member wants

He is interested in what kind of mind you have and how it works – not in playing games. Furthermore, he can usually spot this practice and will actually grade you down on it.

13) Do not switch sides in your reply merely to agree with a board member

Frequently, a member will take a contrary position merely to draw you out and to see if you are willing and able to defend your point of view. Do not start a debate, yet do not surrender a good position. If a position is worth taking, it is worth defending.

14) Do not be afraid to admit an error in judgment if you are shown to be wrong

The board knows that you are forced to reply without any opportunity for careful consideration. Your answer may be demonstrably wrong. If so, admit it and get on with the interview.

15) Do not dwell at length on your present job

The opening question may relate to your present assignment. Answer the question but do not go into an extended discussion. You are being examined for a *new* job, not your present one. As a matter of fact, try to phrase ALL your answers in terms of the job for which you are being examined.

Basis of Rating

Probably you will forget most of these "do's" and "don'ts" when you walk into the oral interview room. Even remembering them all will not ensure you a passing grade. Perhaps you did not have the qualifications in the first place. But remembering them will help you to put your best foot forward, without treading on the toes of the board members.

Rumor and popular opinion to the contrary notwithstanding, an oral board wants you to make the best appearance possible. They know you are under pressure – but they also want to see how you respond to it as a guide to what your reaction would be under the pressures of the job you seek. They will be influenced by the degree of poise you display, the personal traits you show and the manner in which you respond.

ABOUT THIS BOOK

This book contains tests divided into Examination Sections. Go through each test, answering every question in the margin. We have also attached a sample answer sheet at the back of the book that can be removed and used. At the end of each test look at the answer key and check your answers. On the ones you got wrong, look at the right answer choice and learn. Do not fill in the answers first. Do not memorize the questions and answers, but understand the answer and principles involved. On your test, the questions will likely be different from the samples. Questions are changed and new ones added. If you understand these past questions you should have success with any changes that arise. Tests may consist of several types of questions. We have additional books on each subject should more study be advisable or necessary for you. Finally, the more you study, the better prepared you will be. This book is intended to be the last thing you study before you walk into the examination room. Prior study of relevant texts is also recommended. NLC publishes some of these in our Fundamental Series. Knowledge and good sense are important factors in passing your exam. Good luck also helps. So now study this Passbook, absorb the material contained within and take that knowledge into the examination. Then do your best to pass that exam.

EXAMINATION SECTION

EXAMINATION SECTION
TEST 1

DIRECTIONS: Each question or incomplete statement is followed by several suggested answers or completions. Select the one that BEST answers the question or completes the statement. *PRINT THE LETTER OF THE CORRECT ANSWER IN THE SPACE AT THE RIGHT.*

1. The one of the following diseases which is the LEADING cause of death in the 10-to-15 year age group is
   A. cancer   B. tuberculosis   C. poliomyelitis
   D. diabetes   E. rheumatic fever

   1.____

2. The one of the following which would MOST likely be a result of untreated syphilis is
   A. paresis   B. phlebitis   C. carcinoma
   D. silicosis   E. angina pectoris

   2.____

3. The one of the following which is MOST likely to be used in establishing a diagnosis of epilepsy is a(n)
   A. electrocardiogram   B. spinal x-ray
   C. fluoroscopic examination D. electroencephalogram
   E. psychometric examination

   3.____

4. The pathology of diabetes involves the FAILURE of the body to produce an adequate supply of
   A. sugar   B. carbohydrates   C. insulin
   D. salt   E. bile

   4.____

5. The one of the following statements that is TRUE about diabetes is that
   A. it can generally be cured if medical orders are followed
   B. it can generally be kept under control but not cured
   C. it is an infectious disease
   D. blindness is an inevitable result of it
   E. controlled diabetes is a progressively disabling disease

   5.____

6. Scurvy is caused by a deficiency of vitamin
   A. A   B. B   C. C   D. E   E. K

   6.____

7. Vitamin D deficiency is common because
   A. it can only be injected
   B. it is generally associated with poorly tasting foods
   C. only physicians can administer it
   D. it is not found naturally in many foods

   7.____

8. The one of the following vitamins that is used as an aid in coagulating blood is vitamin
   A. A   B. B   C. C   D. E   E. K

   8.____

9. The one of the following statements that is TRUE of Duchenne muscular dystrophy is that
   A. it is transmitted to the male children through the mother
   B. the male is the carrier of the disease
   C. the brain is primarily affected because of a lack of blood supply
   D. it is caused by a nutritional deficiency in the antepartum period
   E. only female children are susceptible to the disease

9._____

10. If a patient is repeatedly admitted to the hospital because of a series of mishaps in which he has suffered broken bones, the one of the following that is MOST likely to be true is that he is
    A. a rigid person   B. a diabetic   C. malingering
    D. accident prone   E. psychotic

10._____

11. The one of the following groups of illnesses that is known to be caused by bacteria is
    A. mental diseases   B. acute infectious diseases
    C. nutritional diseases   D. degenerative diseases
    E. cancerous tumors

11._____

12. The one of the following with which Hodgkin's Disease is COMMONLY associated is
    A. neurasthenia   B. meningitis   C. poliomyelitis
    D. cancer   E. tuberculosis

12._____

13. The one of the following diseases in which the determination of the sedimentation rate is IMPORTANT for diagnostic purposes is
    A. rheumatic heart disease   B. congenital heart disease
    C. hypertensive heart disease   D. diabetes
    E. gonorrhea

13._____

14. The one of the following disease classifications that would INCLUDE spinal meningitis is
    A. cancer or tumor   B. nutritional disease
    C. acute infectious disease   D. focal or local infection
    E. acute poisoning or intoxication

14._____

15. The one of the following diseases that may cause visual impairment and blindness is
    A. ringworm   B. osteomyelitis
    C. poliomyelitis   D. gall bladder disease
    E. diabetes

15._____

16. The one of the following that is NOT an anesthetic is
    A. cholesterol   B. nitrous oxide   C. sodium pentothal
    D. procaine   E. ethyl chloride

16._____

17. The one of the following that BEST describes the restrictions to be applied to Mr. K., a cardiac patient classified, according to the standards of the American Heart Association, as functional, Class IVD, is
    A. limited activity
    B. complete bed rest
    C. four hours rest daily
    D. prohibition of stair climbing, alcohol or tobacco
    E. convalescent status

17.____

18. Over time, geriatrics has become an increasingly important branch of medicine CHIEFLY due to
    A. greater specialization within the medical profession
    B. the discovery of penicillin and aureomycin
    C. advances in medical education
    D. increases in hospitalization
    E. the increase in the span of life

18.____

19. The one of the following which is MOST likely to be an occupational disease is
    A. cancer   B. cerebral hemorrhage
    C. septicemia   D. asthma
    E. nephritis

19.____

20. The one of the following that is a NUTRITIONAL disease is
    A. tuberculosis   B. scurvy   C. hepatitis
    D. lymphoma   E. scabies

20.____

21. Morbidity rate refers to the
    A. incidence of an illness
    B. ratio of births to deaths
    C. bacterial count
    D. degree of disability caused by an illness
    E. death rate

21.____

22. A pediatrician is a doctor who specializes in the treatment of
    A. children   B. foot diseases
    C. disabling illnesses   D. orthopedic diseases
    E. the aged

22.____

23. A sadistic person is one who
    A. receives gratification through suffering pain
    B. secures a great deal of satisfaction from his own body
    C. receives gratification from inflicting pain on others
    D. turns all feelings towards others back into his own personality
    E. seeks solace through deep mental depression

23.____

24. The one of the following which is said to be the masculine counterpart of the *Electra Complex* is the _____ complex.
    A. sexual perversion   B. frustration   C. Oedipus
    D. reanimation   E. repression

24.____

25. The one of the following conditions for which a patient would be admitted to a state mental hospital is
    A. schizophrenia
    B. muscular dystrophy
    C. pathological lying
    D. congenital syphilis
    E. psychoneurosis

26. The one of the following statements which BEST describes the difference between a hallucination and a delusion is that
    A. hallucinations occur only at night
    B. delusions occur only with menopause
    C. delusions are primarily provoked by sexual function
    D. a hallucination has a basis in beliefs or ideas
    E. a delusion has a basis in beliefs or ideas

27. Finger sucking in early childhood has long been a subject of discussion among psychiatrists.
    The one of the following statements that is GENERALLY accepted as true is that
    A. finger sucking denotes pending neuroses and the parents need psychiatric consultation
    B. finger sucking is a normal activity of early childhood and should not be interfered with
    C. finger sucking alters the child's facial contours and should be heavily discouraged
    D. finger sucking by a child over nine months old is due to emotional upset and needs treatment
    E. the physician should discuss possible remedial measures such as guards on fingers

28. The one of the following who is said to be the *Father of Medicine* is
    A. Hippocrates
    B. Pasteur
    C. Galen
    D. Sydenham
    E. Plato

29. The one of the following who is credited with the improvement of conditions in mental hospitals and the founding of new ones in the United States is
    A. Andrew Jackson
    B. Dorothea Dix
    C. William Knowlton
    D. Robert Stack
    E. Rene Laennec

30. The one of the following doctors whose name is COMMONLY associated with much of the early growth and subsequent progress of medical social work is Dr.
    A. Sigmund Freud
    B. Richard C. Cabot
    C. Elizabeth Blackwell
    D. Carmyn Lombardo
    E. Thomas Parran

KEY (CORRECT ANSWERS)

1.	A	11.	B	21.	A
2.	A	12.	D	22.	A
3.	D	13.	A	23.	C
4.	C	14.	C	24.	C
5.	B	15.	E	25.	A
6.	C	16.	A	26.	E
7.	D	17.	B	27.	B
8.	E	18.	E	28.	A
9.	A	19.	D	29.	B
10.	D	20.	B	30.	B

EXAMINATION SECTION
TEST 1

DIRECTIONS: Each question or incomplete statement is followed by several suggested answers or completions. Select the one that BEST answers the question or completes the statement. *PRINT THE LETTER OF THE CORRECT ANSWER IN THE SPACE AT THE RIGHT.*

1. The one of the following which is the BEST reason for a medical social worker's having a sound foundation of medical information is that she may be able to

    A. determine the degree of disability which each illness may cause
    B. assist the doctors in bringing about solutions to medical problems
    C. instruct visiting nurses in case work
    D. instruct patients in the proper way to carry out medical recommendations
    E. work intelligently as a member of the medical team in helping sick people make the best use of medical care

    1.____

2. The one of the following which a medical social worker should consider the LEAST desirable during the course of the treatment interview with the client is to

    A. foster a totally dependent attitude
    B. respect the client's judgment
    C. permit the client to talk about possible solutions
    D. respect the client as an individual person
    E. clear the air and let the client talk

    2.____

3. The one of the following which is MOST likely to be the medical social worker's role with a clinic patient who has a mild case of diabetes is to

    A. help the patient change his environment
    B. help the patient accept his illness
    C. arrange for the placement of his children
    D. arrange for blood sugar tests
    E. arrange convalescent care

    3.____

4. The one of the following which is the PRIMARY purpose of the teaching of medical students by a medical social worker is to

    A. impress upon them the responsibilities of the medical social worker
    B. increase the number of referrals to the medical social worker
    C. make them aware of the social and emotional factors which may complicate the care of patients
    D. describe the development of social work to them
    E. teach them medical social casework

    4.____

5. The one of the following functions which is agreed by medical social work authorities to be the PROPER focus of a modern medical social service department is

    A. teaching social aspects of medicine
    B. assisting in research
    C. providing medical relief
    D. completing brief service cases
    E. performing casework

    5.____

7

6. Medical social work authorities consider a 100% review of a diagnostic group in a hospital an appropriate activity of a medical social worker under certain circumstances PROVIDED the purpose is

    A. individualization
    B. health education
    C. transference
    D. steering
    E. medical follow-up

6.___

7. In addition to basic knowledge of social work, the one of the following in which medical social workers are expected to have SPECIAL ability is

    A. recognizing the symptoms of early illness
    B. first aid
    C. follow-up of tuberculosis contacts
    D. working in a team-work relationship with other professions in a medical agency
    E. planning recreation programs in hospital wards

7.___

8. The administrator of a hospital is responsible for the total functioning of the institution, and each department head is responsible to the administrator for the proper functioning of his department. Assuming that you are a medical social worker in the hospital and a student nurse is extremely insolent to you or to a patient in your presence, the one of the following to whom you should report her action is

    A. the doctor on service
    B. the director of nurses
    C. your immediate supervisor
    D. the registered nurse on the floor
    E. the hospital administrator

8.___

9. An acutely ill mother of a healthy two-week old infant girl is admitted to a hospital at night. The following morning, the husband of the patient phones the medical social worker on the service and demands to know why the baby was refused readmission to the hospital nursery when it only left there the week before.
The one of the following replies which the medical social worker SHOULD give to the husband is that

    A. there are no vacant bassinets in the nursery
    B. the baby was not admitted to the nursery because she is not sick
    C. if social service had been on duty, the baby would have been admitted
    D. he should report the matter to the medical superintendent
    E. infants are never admitted to the nursery from outside the hospital

9.___

10. The one of the following which is the PRIMARY role of social casework is to

    A. direct people who have little knowledge of life toward more satisfying experiences
    B. readjust environmental factors which are hindering a person's social adjustment
    C. help people recognize and handle problems which are not beyond their capacity to solve
    D. give sympathetic understanding to individuals who have social problems
    E. refer individuals to the proper community resource to meet their needs

10.___

11. The one of the following which is the PRIME requisite of a good social worker is a

    A. respect for the worth of an individual
    B. high degree of intelligence
    C. knowledge of psychiatry and mental hygiene
    D. sound knowledge of resources
    E. good knowledge of human behavior

12. Of the following, the one which is the BEST definition of social casework is

    A. a substitute for proper family relations
    B. a treatment process for sick persons
    C. a method of mass treatment of social problems
    D. an individual approach to people in trouble
    E. a method of solving financial problems

13. The one of the following which may be said to have come FIRST in the history and development of social work as a profession is

    A. analytical assistance
    B. friendly visiting by volunteer workers
    C. psychological approach
    D. outdoor relief
    E. social diagnoses

14. The one of the following circumstances in which casework service would be MOST likely to bring about a *successful* solution is in a situation in which

    A. a family is satisfied with things as they are
    B. the attitudes and habits of a patient are firmly entrenched and of long standing
    C. for one reason or another, there is only financial need
    D. the worker is working for the community against the desires of the patient
    E. a family seeks help with the problem of an adolescent child

15. The one of the following which is an IDEAL social casework situation is a(n)

    A. prisoner released from a reformatory who is very penitent for his crime
    B. person who is pronounced cured of congenital syphilis
    C. unwed mother who is seeking assistance by court action to punish the putative father
    D. psychoneurotic patient who is aware that her problems come from within her environment and her reaction to this environment
    E. person who knows he needs help, is capable of cooperating, and seeks some solution to his problem

16. In distinguishing between functions of a public agency and a private agency, the one of the following functions which would MOST likely belong only to a private agency is to

    A. investigate occupational resources
    B. investigate need for complete financial assistance
    C. evaluate need of an individual for rehabilitation
    D. do casework with the marginal income group
    E. determine budgetary needs of the indigent group

17. The one of the following services to patients which is not considered as legitimately falling within the functions of the medical social service department of a hospital is the

    A. securing of appliances
    B. arranging for convalescent care
    C. arranging for day care for children
    D. dispensing of medications
    E. reporting to community agencies

18. A voluntary hospital is a hospital

    A. in which doctors are forbidden to accept fees
    B. which accepts only patients unable to pay the full cost of their care
    C. which is entirely supported by public contributions
    D. in which most of the hospital workers are volunteers
    E. which is a non-profit institution

19. The one of the following which is a TRUE statement regarding the commissioner of hospitals is that he is

    A. responsible for the health of all residents of the city
    B. appointed by the mayor
    C. required to sign all commitment papers
    D. responsible only to the governor of the state
    E. an elected official for a two-year term

20. The one of the following which is a TRUE statement is that medical care in a tax-supported hospital is available to

    A. only those who have settlement in the area
    B. only those receiving public assistance
    C. all persons in need of medical treatment
    D. emergency cases only
    E. persons with contagious diseases only

21. The one of the following which is the PRIMARY function of the department of health is

    A. the treatment of contagious diseases
    B. education of the public towards better health
    C. conducting statistical research in problems of health
    D. providing nursing service to the indigent
    E. the distribution of health literature

22. A premarital blood test is required prior to the issuance of a marriage license. This requirement may be waived when

    A. both parties have been married before to different spouses
    B. the woman is pregnant at the time the marriage license is requested
    C. both parties have had physical examinations by a private physician
    D. both parties present reports of negative blood tests taken 6 months prior to the request for a license
    E. the man is over 65 years of age and in apparent good health

23. The one of the following statements regarding the care and treatment of tuberculous patients in the state which is FALSE is:

    A. If it is established that an alien was suffering from tuberculosis at the time of landing or becomes a public charge as a result of this condition within five years, he is eligible for sanitarium care for a one-year period in a federal hospital
    B. Any person affected with a communicable disease such as tuberculosis, likely to be dangerous to the lives and health of other persons, may be removed to a hospital designated by a board of health, upon the report of a duly authorized physician
    C. Care and treatment provided by the state or by any county or city for persons suffering from tuberculosis shall be available without cost or charge to any person having state residence and at the discretion of the state commissioner of health to any other person in the state who is suffering from tuberculosis
    D. Persons approved for admission to state hospitals unable to pay for transportation may be furnished such transportation by the superintendent of the hospital, and that transportation to another hospital for special care and treatment may also be furnished
    E. Any person who volunteers to assume and pay for the cost of the care and treatment of a patient suffering from tuberculosis shall be permitted to do so, but no state, county, city, or other public official shall request or require such payment

24. The one of the following which forms a PRIMARY aim of school child guidance clinics is the

    A. treatment of the parents
    B. prevention of juvenile delinquency
    C. prevention of mental ill health
    D. prevention of truancy
    E. treatment of the narcotic addict

25. The Community Chest and the Council of Social Agencies in cities where both exist work cooperatively to provide the greatest welfare for the entire community. The one of the following functions which would fall EXCLUSIVELY within the functions of the Community Chest is to

    A. give group work service to the community
    B. provide recreational facilities to members
    C. support agency functions and programs
    D. raise funds for the social welfare and health agencies
    E. interpret the work of individual agencies

26. The one of the following which is the PRIMARY function of the Tuberculosis and Health Association is

    A. psychometric testing
    B. convalescent care
    C. education of the public
    D. financial assistance
    E. surgical treatment

27. The one of the following which is the CHIEF purpose of the visits paid by a public health nurse to a patient in his home is to

    A. educate patient or patient group to give adequate care
    B. make epidemiological investigations
    C. report to the truant authority
    D. give reassurance to patient and patient group
    E. evaluate the home situation for emotional and physical strains

28. When a post-partum patient and her baby are discharged after a week in a hospital and the case is referred to the Visiting Nurse Service, the one of the following which is the USUAL routine for the visiting nurse is to

    A. visit daily for the next week to check on the mother's condition and to bathe the baby
    B. arrange for housekeeping service if it seems necessary
    C. keep in touch with the nurse in the school attended by other children in the family to avoid exposing the baby to a communicable disease
    D. keep the referral on file unless the patient is under a physician's care at home
    E. visit within a short time of the patient's return home to instruct her in the care of the baby

29. A 35-year-old woman who had always lived in New York City was diagnosed as having osteomyelitis of the left tibia, and was admitted to a New York City hospital for treatment. Conservative treatment was of no avail, and she had an amputation below the left knee. The medical social worker was called in to see her as she said she had spent five months in San Francisco, California, just prior to her hospitalization and had no means of support. She needed an artificial leg before leaving the hospital, plus financial support. Before her illness, she was a typist.
    The one of the following agencies which should be contacted FIRST is the

    A. New York State Department of Social Services
    B. California State Department of Welfare
    C. New York State Division of Vocational Rehabilitation
    D. Welfare Council of New York City
    E. Rehabilitation Division of the New York City Department of Hospitals

30. When the woman described in the preceding question was ready to leave the hospital and the medical social worker was seeking financial support for maintenance, the one of the following agencies which SHOULD be contacted is the

    A. Department of Social Services
    B. Florence Crittenton League
    C. Division of Placement and Unemployment Insurance
    D. Workmen's Compensation Office
    E. Community Service Society

31. The name of the following institutions which is NOT under the management and control of the State Department of Correction is the   31.____

    A. Berkshire Industrial Farm
    B. Wallkill Prison
    C. Woodbourne Correctional Institution
    D. Elmira Reformatory
    E. State Vocational Institution

32. The one of the following which can be considered the PRIMARY purpose of the Social Security Act is the   32.____

    A. insurance against loss of earnings by an injured employee
    B. furthering of the security of the citizen and his family through social insurance
    C. distribution of surplus wealth among the needy classes
    D. development of an economic balance between the wealthy and the poor
    E. insurance of dependents against need

33. The passage of the Social Security Act in 1935 points toward the establishment of a broad national welfare program. The one of the following ways in which federal funds are provided, according to the provisions of the Act, is through   33.____

    A. payment of all the administrative funds used in disbursing state and local funds
    B. maintenance of adequate institutions to foster a good national program
    C. lump sum payments to all needy blind and widows
    D. part payment in participation with state and local funds
    E. full payment to individual recipients

34. The one of the following groups of persons which is ELIGIBLE for benefits under the Social Security Act is   34.____

    A. persons who have worked a required period of time in certain covered occupations
    B. the dependents of workmen injured or killed while on the job
    C. all those over 65 years old who are unable to find employment
    D. the dependents of soldiers, sailors, or marines killed while on combat duty
    E. all citizens who have reached the age of 65 years, whether or not in need of financial assistance

35. Of the following categories, the one which was MOST recently added to those which are covered under the Social Security Act is   35.____

    A. the blind   B. the permanently disabled
    C. crippled adults   D. the aged
    E. dependent children

KEY (CORRECT ANSWERS)

1. E	11. A	21. B	31. A
2. A	12. D	22. B	32. B
3. B	13. B	23. A	33. D
4. C	14. E	24. C	34. A
5. E	15. E	25. D	35. B
6. A	16. D	26. C	
7. D	17. D	27. A	
8. C	18. E	28. E	
9. E	19. B	29. C	
10. C	20. C	30. A	

EXAMINATION SECTION
TEST 1

DIRECTIONS: Each question or incomplete statement is followed by several suggested answers or completions. Select the one that *BEST* answers the question or completes the statement. *PRINT THE LETTER OF THE CORRECT ANSWER IN THE SPACE AT THE RIGHT.*

1. When a counselor is planning a future interview with a client, of the following, the *MOST* important consideration is the

    A. recommendations he will make to the client
    B. place where the client will be interviewed
    C. purpose for which the client will be interviewed
    D. personality of the client

2. For a counselor to make a practice of reviewing the client's case record, if available, prior to the interview, is, usually,

    A. *inadvisable,* because knowledge of the client's past record will tend to influence the counselor's judgment
    B. *advisable,* because knowledge of the client's background will help the counselor to identify discrepancies in the client's responses
    C. *inadvisable,* because such review is time-consuming and of questionable value
    D. *advisable,* because knowledge of the client's background will help the counselor to understand the client's situation

3. Assume that a counselor makes a practice of constantly reassuring clients with serious and complex problems by making such statements as: "I'm sure you'll soon be well;" "I know you'll get a job soon;" or "Everything will be all right."
Of the following, the *MOST* likely result of such a practice is to

    A. encourage the client and make him feel that the counselor understands what the client is going through
    B. make the client doubtful about the counselor's understanding of his difficulties and the counselor's ability to help
    C. confuse the client and cause him to hesitate to take any action on his own initiative
    D. help the client to be more realistic about his situation and the probability that it will improve

4. In order to get the maximum amount of information from a client during an interview, of the following, it is *MOST* important for the counselor to communicate to the client the feeling that the counselor is

    A. interested in the client
    B. a figure of authority
    C. efficient in his work habits
    D. sympathetic to the client's lifestyle

5. Of the following, the counselor who takes extremely detailed notes during an interview with a client is *most likely* to

    A. encourage the client to talk freely

B. distract and antagonize the client
C. help the client feel at ease
D. understand the client's feelings

6. As a counselor, you find that many of the clients you interview are verbally abusive and unusually hostile to you.
   Of the following, the MOST appropriate action for you to take first is to

   A. review your interviewing techniques and consider whether you may be provoking these clients
   B. act in a more authoritative manner when interviewing troublesome clients
   C. tell these clients that you will not process their applications unless their troublesome behavior ceases
   D. disregard the clients' troublesome behavior during the interview

7. During an interview, you did not completely understand several of your client's responses. In each instance, you rephrased the client's statement and asked the client if that was what he meant.
   For you to use such a technique during interviews would be considered

   A. *inappropriate;* you may have distorted the client's meaning by rephrasing his statements
   B. *inappropriate;* you should have asked the same questioE until you received a comprehensible response
   C. *appropriate;* the client will have a chance to correct you if you have misinterpreted his responses
   D. *appropriate;* a counselor should rephrase clients' responses for the records

8. A counselor is interviewing a client who has just had a severe emotional shock because of an assault on her by a mugger.
   Of the following, the approach which would generally be MOST helpful to the client is for the counselor to

   A. comfort the client and encourage her to talk about the assault
   B. sympathize with the client but refuse to discuss the assault with her
   C. tell the client to control her emotions and think positively about the future
   D. proceed with the interview in an impersonal and unemotional manner

9. A counselor finds that her questions are misinterpreted by many of the clients she interviews.
   Of the following, the MOST likely reason for this problem is that the

   A. client is not listening attentively
   B. client wants to avoid the subject being discussed
   C. counselor has failed to express her meaning clearly
   D. counselor has failed to put the client at ease

10. For a counselor to look directly at the client and observe him during the interview is generally

    A. *inadvisable;* this will make the client nervous and uncomfortable
    B. *advisable;* the client will be more likely to refrain from lying
    C. *inadvisable;* the counselor will not be able to take notes for the case record
    D. *advisable;* this will encourage conversation and accelerate the progress of the interview

11. You are interviewing a client who is applying for social services for the first time. In order to encourage this client to freely give you the information needed for you to establish his eligibility, of the following, the BEST way to start the interview is by

    A. asking questions the client can easily answer
    B. conveying the impression that his responses to your questions will be checked
    C. asking two or three similar but important questions
    D. assuring the client that your sole responsibility is "getting the facts"

12. Counselors are encouraged to record significant information obtained from clients and services provided for clients. Of the following, the MOST important reason for this practice is that these case records will

    A. help to reduce the need for regular supervisory conferences
    B. indicate to counselors which clients are taking up the most time
    C. provide information which will help the agency to improve its services to clients
    D. make it easier to verify the complaints of clients

13. As a counselor you find that interviews can be completed in a shorter period of time if you ask questions which limit the client to a certain answer.
    For you to use such a technique would be considered

    A. *inappropriate,* because this type of question usually requires advance preparation
    B. *inappropriate,* because this type of question may inhibit the client from saying what he really means
    C. *appropriate,* because you know the areas into which the questions should be directed
    D. *appropriate,* because this type of question usually helps clients to express themselves clearly

14. Assume that, while you are interviewing an individual to obtain information, the individual pauses in the middle of an answer.
    The BEST of the following actions for you to take at this time is to

    A. correct any inaccuracies in what he has said
    B. remain silent until he continues
    C. explain your position on the matter being discussed
    D. explain that time is short and that he must complete his story quickly

15. You have been assigned to interview the mother of a five-year-old son in her home to get information useful in locating the child's absent father. During the interview, you notice many serious bruises on the child's arms and legs, which the mother explains are due to the child's clumsiness. Of the following, your BEST course of action is to

    A. accept the mother's explanation and concentrate on getting information which will help you to locate the father
    B. advise the mother to have the child examined for a medical condition that may be causing his clumsiness
    C. make a surprise visit to the mother later, to see if someone is beating the child
    D. complete your interview with the mother and report the case to your supervisor for investigation of possible child abuse

16. During an interview, the former landlord of an absent father offers to help you to locate the father if you will give the landlord confidential information you have on the financial situation of the father.
    Of the following, you should

    A. immediately end the interview with the landlord
    B. urge the landlord to help you but explain that you are not permitted to give him confidential information
    C. freely give the landlord the confidential information he requests about the father
    D. give the landlord the information only if he promises to keep it confidential

17. You feel that your client, a released mental patient, is not adjusting well to living on his own in an apartment. To gather more information, you interview privately his next-door neighbor, who claims that the client is creating a "disturbance" and speaks of the client in an angry and insulting manner.
    Of the following, the BEST action for you to take in this situation is to

    A. listen patiently to the neighbor to try to get the facts about your client's behavior
    B. inform the neighbor that he has no right to speak insultingly about a mentally ill person
    C. make an appointment to interview the neighbor some other time when he isn't so upset
    D. tell the neighbor that you were not aware of the client's behavior and that you will have the client moved

18. As a counselor, you are interviewing a client to determine his eligibility for a work program. Suddenly the client begins to shout that he is in no condition to work and that you are persecuting him for no reason.
    Of the following, your BEST response to this client is to

    A. advise the client to stop shouting or you will call for the security guard
    B. wait until the client calms down, then order him to come back for another interview
    C. insist that you are not persecuting the client and that he must complete the interview
    D. wait until the client calms down, say that you understand how he feels, and try to continue the interview

19. You are interviewing a mother whose 17-year-old son has recently been returned home from a mental institution. Although she is willing to care for her son at home, she is frightened by his strange and sometimes violent behavior and does not know the best arrangement to make for his care.
    Of the following, your MOST appropriate response to this mother's problem is to

    A. describe the supportive services and alternatives to home care which are available
    B. help her to accept her son's strange and violent behavior
    C. tell her that she will not be permitted to care for her son at home if she is frightened by his behavior
    D. convince her that she is not responsible for her son's mental condition

20. Assume that you are interviewing an elderly man who comes to the center several times a month to discuss topics with you which are not related to social services. You realize that the man is lonely and enjoys these conversations.
    Of the following, it would be MOST appropriate to

    A. politely discourage the man from coming in to pass the time with you
    B. avoid speaking to this man the next time he comes into the center
    C. explore with the client his feelings about joining a senior citizens' center
    D. continue to hold these conversations with the man

21. A client you are interviewing tends to ramble on after each response that he gives, so that many clients are kept waiting.
    In this situation, of the following, it would be MOST advisable to

    A. try to direct the interview, in order to obtain the necessary information
    B. reduce the number of questions asked so that you can shorten the interview
    C. arrange a second interview for the client so that you can give him more time
    D. tell the client that he is wasting everybody's time

22. A non-minority counselor is about to interview a minority client on public assistance for job placement when the client says: "What does your kind know about my problems? You've never had to survive out on these streets."
    Of the following, the counselor's MOST appropriate response in this situation is to

    A. postpone the interview until a minority counselor is available to interview the client
    B. tell the client that he must cooperate with the counselor if he wants to continue receiving public assistance
    C. explain to the client the function of the counselor in this unit and the services he provides
    D. assure the client that you do not have to be a member of a minority group to understand the effects of poverty

23. When you are interviewing someone to obtain information, the BEST of the following reasons for you to repeat certain of his exact words is to

    A. *assure* him that appropriate action will be taken
    B. *encourage* him to elaborate on a point he has made
    C. *assure* him that you agree with his point of view
    D. *encourage* him to switch to another topic of discussion

24. You are interviewing a young client who seriously under-estimates the amount of education and training he will require for a certain occupation.
    For you to tell the client that you think he is mistaken would generally be considered

    A. *inadvisable*, because counselors should not express their opinions to clients
    B. *inadvisable*, because clients have the right to self-determination
    C. *advisable*, because clients should generally be alerted to their misconceptions
    D. *advisable*, because counselors should convince clients to adopt a proper life style

25. Of the following, the MOST appropriate manner for a counselor to assume during an interview with a patient is

    A. authoritarian
    B. paternal
    C. casual
    D. businesslike

KEY (CORRECT ANSWERS)

1.	C	11.	A
2.	D	12.	C
3.	B	13.	B
4.	A	14.	B
5.	B	15.	D
6.	A	16.	B
7.	C	17.	A
8.	A	18.	D
9.	C	19.	A
10.	D	20.	C

21. A
22. C
23. B
24. C
25. D

TEST 2

DIRECTIONS: Each question or incomplete statement is followed by several suggested answers or completions. Select the one that *BEST* answers the question or completes the statement. *PRINT THE LETTER OF THE CORRECT ANSWER IN THE SPACE AT THE RIGHT.*

1. You are interviewing a legally responsible absent father who refuses to make child support payments because he claims the mother physically abuses the child.
Of the following, the *BEST* way for you to handle this situation is to tell the father that you

    A. will report his complaint about the mother, but he is still responsible for making child support payments
    B. suspect that he is complaining about the mother in order to avoid his own responsibility for making child support payments
    C. are concerned with his responsibility to make child support payments, not with the mother's abuse of the child
    D. can not determine his responsibility for making child support payments until his complaint about the mother is investigated

2. You are interviewing an elderly woman who lives alone to determine her eligibility for homemaker service at public expense. Though obviously frail and in need of this service, the woman is not completely cooperative, and during the interview, is often silent for a considerable period of time.
Of the following, the *BEST* way for you to deal with these periods of silence is to

    A. realize that she may be embarrassed to have to apply for homemaker service at public expense, and emphasize her right to this service
    B. postpone the interview and make an appointment with her for a later date, when she may be better able to cooperate
    C. explain to the woman that you have many clients to interview and need her cooperation to complete the interview quickly
    D. recognize that she is probably hiding something and begin to ask questions to draw her out

3. During a conference with an adolescent boy at a juvenile detention center, you find out for the first time that he would prefer to be placed in foster care rather than return to his natural parents.
To uncover the reasons why the boy dislikes his own home, of the following, it would be *MOST* advisable for you to

    A. ask the boy a number of short, simple questions about his feelings
    B. encourage the boy to talk freely and express his feelings as best he can
    C. interview the parents and find out why the boy doesn't want to live at home
    D. administer a battery of psychological tests in order to make an assessment of the boy's problems

4. You are interviewing a mother who is applying for Aid to Families with Dependent Children because the husband has deserted the family. The mother becomes annoyed at having to answer your questions and tells you to leave her apartment.
Which one of the following actions would be *most appropriate* to take *FIRST* in this situation?

A. Return to the office and close the case for lack of cooperation
B. Tell the mother that you will get the information from her neighbors if she does not cooperate
C. Tell the mother that you must stay until you get answers to your questions
D. Explain to the mother the reasons for the interview and the consequences of Her failure to cooperate

5. A counselor counseling juvenile clients finds that, although he can tolerate most of their behavior, he becomes infuriated when they lie to him.
Of the following, the counselor can BEST deal with his anger at his clients' lying by

   A. recognizing his feelings of anger and learning to control expression of these feelings to his clients
   B. warning his clients that he cannot be responsible for his anger when a client lies to him
   C. using will power to suppress his feelings of anger when a client lies to him
   D. realizing that lying is a common trait of juveniles and not directed against him personally

6. During an interview, one of your clients, a former drug addict, has expressed an interest in attending a community counseling center and resuming his education.
In this case, the MOST appropriate action that you should take FIRST is to

   A. determine whether this ambition is realistic for a former drug addict
   B. send the client's application to a community counseling center which provides services to former addicts
   C. ask the client whether he is really motivated or is just seeking your approval
   D. encourage and assist the client to take this step, since his interest is a positive sign

7. You are interviewing a client who, during previous appointments, has not responded to your requests for information required to determine his continued eligibility for services. On this occasion, the client again offers an excuse which you feel is not acceptable.
For you to advise the client of the probable loss of services because of his lack of cooperation is

   A. *inappropriate,* because the threat to withhold services will harm the relationship between counselor and client
   B. *inappropriate,* because counselors should not reveal to clients that they do not believe their statements
   C. *appropriate,* because social services are a reward given to cooperative clients
   D. *appropriate,* beca,us.e the counselor should Inform clients of the consequences of their lack of cooperation

8. Assume that you are counselling an adolescent boy in a juvenile detention center who has been a ringleader in smuggling "pot" into the center.
During your regular interview with this boy, of the following, it would be *advisable* to

   A. tell him you know that he has been involved in smuggling pot and that you are trying to understand the reasons for his misbehavior
   B. ignore his pot smuggling in order to reassure him that you understand and accept him, even though you do not agree with his standards of behavior
   C. warn him that you have reported his pot smuggling and that he will be punished for his misbehavior
   D. show him that you disapprove of his pot smuggling, but assure him that you will not report him for his misbehavior

9. Your unit has received several complaints about a homeless elderly woman living outdoors in various locations in the area. To help determine the need for protective services for this woman, you interview several persons in the neighborhood who are familiar with her, but all are uncooperative or reluctant to give information.
Of the following, your BEST approach to these persons is to explain to them that

   A. you will take legal steps against them if they do not cooperate with you
   B. their cooperation may enable you to help this homeless woman
   C. you need their cooperation to remove this homeless woman from their neighborhood
   D. they will be responsible for any harm that comes to this homeless woman

10. Assume that you are interviewing a client regarding an adjustment in budget. The client begins to scream at you that she holds you responsible for the decrease in her allowance.
Of the following, which is the BEST way for you to handle this situation?

   A. Attempt to discuss the matter calmly with the client and explain her right to a hearing
   B. Urge the client to appeal and assure her of your support
   C. Tell the client that her disorderly behavior will be held against her
   D. Tell the client that the reduction is "due to red tape" and is not your fault

11. As a counselor assigned to a juvenile detention center, you are having a counselling interview with a recently admitted boy who is having serious problems in adjusting to confinement in the center. During the interview, the boy frequently interrupts to ask you personal questions. Of the following, the BEST way for you to deal with these questions is to

   A. tell him in a friendly way that your job is to discuss his problems, not yours
   B. try to understand how the questions relate to the boy's own problems and reply with discretion
   C. take no notice of the questions and continue with the interview
   D. try to win the boy's confidence by answering his questions in detail

12. A counselor is interviewing an elderly woman who hesitates to provide necessary information about her finances to determine whether she is eligible for supplementary assistance. She fears that this information will be reported to others and that her neighbors will find out that she is destitute and applying for "welfare." Of the following, the counselor's MOST appropriate response is to

   A. tell her that, if she hesitates to give this information, the agency will get it from other sources
   B. assure her that this information is kept strictly confidential and will not be given to unauthorized persons
   C. convince her that her application will be turned down unless she provides this information as soon as possible
   D. ask for the name and address of her nearest relative and obtain the information from that person

13. You are counseling a couple whose children have been placed in a foster home because of the couple's quarreling and child neglect. When you interview the wife by herself, she tells you that she knows the husband often "cheats" on her with other women, but she is too afraid of the husband's temper to tell him how much this hurts her.
For you to immediately reveal to the husband the wife's unhappiness concerning his "cheating" is, generally,

    A. *good practice,* because it will help the husband to understand why his wife quarrels with him
    B. *poor practice,* because information received from the wife should not be given to the husband without her permission
    C. *good practice,* because the husband will direct his anger at you rather than at his wife
    D. *poor practice,* because the wife may have told you a false story about her husband in order to win your sympathy

14. A counselor is beginning a job placement interview with a tall, strongly built young man. As the man sits down, the counselor comments: "I know a big fellow like you wouldn't be interested in any clerical job."
For the counselor to make such a comment is, generally,

    A. *appropriate,* because it creates an air of familiarity which may put the man at ease
    B. *inappropriate,* because the man may be sensitive about his physical size
    C. *appropriate,* because, the counselor is using his judgment to help speed up the interview
    D. *inappropriate,* because the man may feel he is being pressured into agreeing with the counselor

15. A counselor in a men's shelter is counseling a middle-aged client for alcoholism. During counseling, the" client confesses that, many years ago, he had often enjoyed sexually abusing his ten-year-old daughter. The counselor tells the client that he personally finds the client's behavior "morally disgusting."
For the counselor to tell the client this is, generally,

    A. *acceptable counseling practice,* because it may encourage the client to feel guilty about his behavior
    B. *unacceptable couseling practice,* because the client may try to shock the counselor by confessing other similar behavior
    C. *acceptable counseling practice,* because "letting off steam" in this manner may relieve tension between the counselor and the client
    D. *unacceptable counseling practice,* because the client may hesitate to discuss his behavior frankly with the counselor in the future

16. During an interview, your client, who wants to move to a larger apartment, asks you to decide on a suitable neighborhood for her.
    For you to make such a decision for the client would, generally, be considered

    A. *appropriate,* because you can save time and expense by sharing your knowledge of neighborhoods with the client
    B. *inappropriate,* because counselors should not help clients with this type of decision
    C. *appropriate,* because this will help the client to develop confidence in her ability to make decisions
    D. *inappropriate,* because the client should be encouraged to accept the responsibility of making this decision

17. A client tells you that he is extremely upset by the treatment that he received from Center personnel at the information desk.
    Which of the following is the BEST way to handle this complaint during the interview?

    A. Explain to the client that he probably misinterpreted what occurred at the information desk
    B. Let the client express his feelings and then proceed with the interview
    C. Tell the client that you are not concerned with the personnel at the information desk
    D. Escort the client to the information desk to find out what really happened

18. You are finishing an interview with a client in which you have explained to her the procedure she must go through to apply for income maintenance.
    Of the following, the BEST way for you to make sure that she has fully understood the procedure is to ask her

    A. whether she feels she has understood your explanation of the procedure
    B. whether she has any questions to ask you about the procedure
    C. to describe the procedure to you in her own words
    D. a few questions to test her understanding of the procedure

19. You are interviewing a client in his home as part of your investigation of an anonymous complaint that he has been receiving Medicaid fraudulently. During the interview, the client frequently interrupts your questions to discuss the hardships of his life and the bitterness he feels about his medical condition.
    Of the following, the BEST way for you to deal with these discussions is to

    A. cut them off abruptly, since the client is probably just trying to avoid answering your questions
    B. listen patiently, since these discussions may be helpful to the client and may give you information for your investigation
    C. remind the client that you are investigating a complaint against him and he must answer directly
    D. seek to gain the client's confidence by discussing any personal or medical problems which you yourself may have

20. While interviewing an absent father to determine his ability to pay child supprt, you realize that his answers to some of your questions contradict his answers to other questions. Of the following, the BEST way for you to try to get accurate information from the father is to

    A. confront him with his contradictory answers and demand an explanation from him
    B. use your best judgment as to which of his answers are accurate and question him accordingly
    C. tell him that he has misunderstood your questions and that he must clarify his answers
    D. ask him the same questions in different words and follow up his answers with related questions

21. The one of the following types of interviewees who presents the LEAST difficult problem to handle is the person who

    A. answers with a great many qualifications
    B. talks at length about unrelated subjects so that the counselor cannot ask questions
    C. has difficulty understanding the counselor's vocabulary
    D. breaks into the middle of sentences and completes them with a meaning of his own

22. A man being interviewed is entitled to Medicaid, but he refuses to sign up for it because he says he cannot accept any form of welfare.
    Of the following, the BEST course of action to take FIRST is to

    A. try to discover the reason for his feeling this way
    B. tell him that he should be glad financial help is available
    C. explain that others cannot help him if he will not help himself
    D. suggest that he speak to someone who is already on Medicaid

23. Of the following, the outcome of an interview by a counselor depends MOST heavily on the

    A. personality of the interviewee
    B. personality of the counselor
    C. subject matter of the questions asked
    D. interaction between counselor and interviewee.

24. Some clients being interviewed are primarily interested in making a favorable impression. The counselor should be aware of the fact that such clients are *more likely* than other clients to

    A. try to anticipate the answers the interviewer is looking for
    B. answer all questions openly and frankly
    C. try to assume the role of interviewer
    D. be anxious to get the interview over as quickly as possible

25. The type of interview which a counselor usually conducts is substantially different from most interviewing situations in all of the following aspects EXCEPT the

    A. setting   B. kinds of clients
    C. techniques employed   D. kinds of problems

KEY (CORRECT ANSWERS)

1.	A	11.	B
2.	A	12.	B
3.	B	13.	B
4.	D	14.	D
5.	A	15.	D
6.	D	16.	D
7.	D	17.	B
8.	A	18.	C
9.	B	19.	B
10.	A	20.	D

21. C
22. A
23. D
24. A
25. C

EXAMINATION SECTION
TEST 1

DIRECTIONS: Each question or incomplete statement is followed by several suggested answers or completions. Select the one that BEST answers the question or completes the statement. *PRINT THE LETTER OF THE CORRECT ANSWER IN THE SPACE AT THE RIGHT.*

1. Which one of the following "suggestions to interviewers" should be AVOIDED?

    A. Encourage the client to verbalize his thoughts and feelings.
    B. Cover as much as possible in each interview.
    C. Don't hesitate to refer the client to someone else who might be more helpful in the situation.
    D. The problem which is presented initially, or the one which seems most obvious, often is not the real one.

2. If it seems clear that disturbance in parents' marital relationships is a major factor in causing a child to be emotionally disturbed, the counselor should

    A. point this out to the parents and tell them that for the welfare of their children, they should resolve their difficulties
    B. suggest that he will be willing to discuss their marital difficulties with them
    C. ignore this and concentrate on helping the child
    D. tactfully suggest that their marital difficulties may be playing a part in their child's disturbance and offer to refer the parents to a qualified marriage counseling service

3. The process of collecting, analyzing, synthesizing and interpreting information about the client should be

    A. completed prior to counseling
    B. completed early in the counseling process
    C. limited to counseling which is primarily diagnostic in purpose
    D. continuous throughout counseling

4. Catharsis, the "emotional unloading" of the client's feelings, has a value in the early stages of counseling because it accomplishes all BUT which one of the following goals?

    A. It relieves strong physiological tensions in the client.
    B. It increases the client's anxiety and therefore his motivation to continue counseling.
    C. It provides a verbal substitute for "acting out" the client's aggressive feelings.
    D. It releases emotional energy which the client has been using to maintain his defenses.

5. During the first interview, the counselor can expect the client to participate at his BEST when the counselor

    A. structures the nature of the counseling process
    B. attempts to summarize the client's problem for him
    C. allows the client to verbalize at his own pace
    D. tells the client that he understands the presenting problem

6. To obtain the most effective results in change of attitude and behavior through parent education, the leader should be

   A. thoroughly grounded in the whole field of psychology
   B. able to help members of the group look at their own attitudes and behavior in constructive ways
   C. completely confident as to the right solution to problems that may be brought up
   D. a warm, charming, friendly human being

7. A social worker's report about a client states that a mother has ambivalent feelings concerning her child. This means that the mother

   A. has contradictory emotional reactions concerning her child
   B. is overprotective of the child
   C. strongly rejects the child
   D. is unduly apprehensive about the child's welfare

8. A psychological report notes, "The client shows little effect." This means that the client

   A. did not take the test too seriously
   B. did not show emotional behavior in situations which normally call for such reactions
   C. did not show signs of fatigue as the testing progressed
   D. reacted to the test situation in a generally favorable manner

9. A psychologist's report states, in part, that a client exhibits some masochistic symptoms. This will be evident to the counselor through the client's persistent attempts at

   A. self-assertion
   B. self-effacement
   C. inflicting physical harm on others
   D. sexual molestation of others of the same sex

10. According to research studies, the type of counselor response that is MOST often followed by a client's expression of insight or illumination is

    A. clarification of feeling
    B. reflection of feeling
    C. simple acceptance
    D. exploratory question

11. Of the following, the BEST way to deal with a 12-year-old boy who feels inferior to his peers is to

    A. provide tasks which he can master with little difficulty
    B. show him how irrational his feelings are
    C. accept his declarations of lack of confidence sympathetically
    D. carefully arrange situations in which he will be obliged to show leadership

12. In counseling or psychotherapy, the factor which is the MOST important for success tends to be the

    A. counselor's theoretical orientation
    B. counselor's attitudes and feelings toward the client

C. techniques used by the counselor
D. amount of experience and training possessed by the counselor

13. Transference is an important aspect of   13.____

    A. test construction   B. grade placement
    C. anecdotal record keeping   D. therapy

14. The MOST desirable way of establishing rapport with a client who comes to the counse-   14.____
    lor with a problem is to

    A. demonstrate sincere interest in him
    B. offer to do everything possible to solve his problem for him
    C. use the language of the client
    D. promise to keep his problem confidential

15. Role playing has been used as a technique in parent education work. Of the following,   15.____
    the major value is that it

    A. permits parents to express unconscious feelings and thereby solve conflicts
    B. tells a story in a forceful and therefore lasting way
    C. provides an opportunity for the individual to view his problems by standing off and looking at them through the eyes of someone else
    D. brings to light problems people never knew they had

16. If during a counseling situation a client expressed anger about a particular situation,   16.____
    which of the following responses would a non-directive counselor MOST likely make?

    A. "Why are you so angry?"
    B. "Is there any need to get so upset about this?"
    C. "This has really made you very mad, hasn't it?"
    D. "Do you feel better now that you have expressed your anger?"

17. In a counseling process, the counselor should usually give information   17.____

    A. whenever it is needed
    B. at the end of the process
    C. in the introductory interview
    D. just before the client would ordinarily request it

18. "After having recognized and clarified feelings and conflicts, it is usually necessary to go   18.____
    beyond the stage of understanding and to elaborate a constructive plan for future action."
    Which of the following people would NOT go along with the above statement?

    A. Thorne   B. Robinson
    C. Williamson   D. Rogers

19. The counselor should focus his attention in the beginning upon   19.____

    A. the transference phenomenon
    B. evidences of hostility
    C. the unique characteristics of the particular relationship at hand
    D. indications of client aggressiveness

20. A recent guidance text that stresses the broad developments of our national heritage, our contemporary social setting, our value patterns, and also the integration into guidance of many disciplines-sociology, anthropology, philosophy, psychology-is

    A. FOUNDATIONS OF GUIDANCE - Miller
    B. GUIDANCE POLICY AND PRACTICE - Mathewson
    C. GUIDANCE IN TODAY'S SCHOOLS - Mortenson & Schmuller
    D. GUIDANCE SERVICES - Humphreys, Traxler & North

21. Which one of the following characteristics of counseling is inconsistent with the others?

    A. Counseling is more than advice-giving.
    B. Counseling involves something more than the solution to an immediate problem.
    C. Counseling concerns itself with attitudes rather than actions.
    D. Counseling involves intellectual rather than emotional attitudes as its basic raw material.

22. One approach to counseling has been labeled "non-directive". The word "non-directive" derives from the fact that, in this approach to counseling, the counselor

    A. does not tell the client what he should do
    B. makes the client responsible for the direction of the course of the interviews
    C. does not make judgments about the behavior of the client
    D. avoids possible areas of threat to the client

23. Of the following personality traits, which would be LEAST essential for an effective counselor to possess?

    A. Extroversion   B. Objectivity
    C. Security   D. Sensitivity

24. Interpretation as a therapeutic tool is considered a hindrance to therapy progress by

    A. orthodox Freudians   B. neo-analysts
    C. Rogerians   D. Adlerians

25. The current interpersonal behavior of the client is probably MOST important as a therapy topic to which two analytic theorists?

    A. Freud and Adler   B. Adler and Rank
    C. Freud and Rank   D. Horney and Sullivan

KEY (CORRECT ANSWERS)

1. B
2. D
3. D
4. B
5. C

6. B
7. A
8. B
9. B
10. C

11. A
12. B
13. D
14. A
15. C

16. C
17. A
18. D
19. C
20. A

21. D
22. B
23. A
24. C
25. D

TEST 2

DIRECTIONS: Each question or incomplete statement is followed by several suggested answers or completions. Select the one that BEST answers the question or completes the statement. *PRINT THE LETTER OF THE CORRECT ANSWER IN THE SPACE AT THE RIGHT.*

1. When a counselor is listening to a client, it is MOST important that he be able to 1.____

    A. show interest and agreement with what the client is saying
    B. paraphrase what the client is saying
    C. understand the significance of what the client is saying
    D. differentiate between fact and fiction in what the client is saying

2. On which one of the following is successful counseling LEAST likely to depend? 2.____

    A. The counselor's theoretical orientation
    B. The counselor's ability to bring the client's feelings and attitudes into the open
    C. The counselor's diagnostic ability
    D. The client's readiness for counseling

3. A client is referred to you for counseling against his will and is suspicious and uncooperative. You should 3.____

    A. explain to him that you cannot help him unless he is prepared to cooperate
    B. explain that you are not taking sides and that you will be impartial
    C. show him that you know how he feels and encourage him to talk about it
    D. explain that you are on his side and will listen sympathetically to anything that he might care to bring up

4. Which one of the following would NOT be considered a basic objective of the first interview between a client and a counselor? 4.____

    A. Beginning a sound counseling relationship
    B. Identifying the client's real problem
    C. Opening up the area of client feelings and attitudes
    D. Clarifying the nature of the counseling process for the client

5. All of the following counselor statements or actions are appropriate techniques for ending an interview EXCEPT 5.____

    A. "Our time is nearly up. Is there something else you have in mind for today?"
    B. "Let's see now. Suppose we go over what we've accomplished today."
    C. Counselor may glance at his watch and say, "When would you like to come in again?"
    D. Counselor may shuffle papers on desk and say, "Now, let's see; when is my next appointment?"

6. It has been recognized in recent literature that the value structure of the individual counselor has what kind of effect on the counseling process? 6.____

    A. Direct
    B. Indirect
    C. Little
    D. None

7. The intensive study of the same individuals over a fairly long period of time represents the
    A. cross-sectional approach
    B. longitudinal approach
    C. clinical approach
    D. biographical approach

8. Of the following techniques, the one which is MOST characteristic of non-directive or client-centered therapy is
    A. encouraging transference
    B. free association
    C. reflection of feeling
    D. permissive questioning

9. In making predictions about how a client will behave in a given situation, a counselor
    A. should limit himself to those situations for which "actuarial" data are available
    B. must rely on "clinical" judgment in many situations but use "actuarial" data wherever possible
    C. should rely on "clinical" judgment in all situations, since they are more valid than "actuarial" predictions
    D. always uses "actuarial" data, but modifies them in light of his "clinical" impression of the client

10. A research study that establishes an hypothesis, sets up control groups, collects data, and generalizes from the data is
    A. formulative
    B. diagnostic
    C. experimental
    D. exploratory

11. The MOST usable single index of the social and economic status of all the members of any family is
    A. occupation of the father
    B. religious affiliation of the family
    C. location of the home in the community
    D. socio-economic rating by neighbors

12. When a counselor does NOT understand the meaning of a response that a counselee has made, the counselor usually should
    A. proceed to another topic
    B. admit his lack of understanding and ask for clarification
    C. act as if he understands so that the counselee's confidence in him is not shaken
    D. ask the counselee to choose his words more carefully

13. When the counselor makes a response which touches off a high degree of resistance in the counselee, he should
    A. apologize and rephrase his remark in a less threatening manner
    B. accept the resistance
    C. ignore the counselee's resistance
    D. recognize that little more will be accomplished in the interview and offer another appointment

14. Directive and non-directive counseling are two emphases in counseling theory and practice. From the pairs of names listed below, indicate the two that are representative of the Directive school.

    A. Thorne and Williamson
    B. Rogers and Thorne
    C. Williamson and Sullivan
    D. Sullivan and Rogers

15. Rogerian counseling theory is based on the assumption that the potential and tendency for growth toward a fully functioning personality is present in

    A. a few "self-actualized" persons
    B. most people of above average intelligence
    C. people whose behavior can be considered as "normal" and socially effective
    D. all people

16. Anecdotal records should contain which type(s) of information?

    A. Evaluations
    B. Interpretations
    C. Factual reports
    D. Prognoses

17. RESISTANCE in relation to psychological counseling typically refers to the

    A. client's defenses against his inner conflicts
    B. counselor's unwillingness to deal with the client's emotional problems
    C. client's having enough ego strength so that he can face his problems
    D. counselor's having enough ego strength so that he can help the client face his problems

18. On which one of the following does the democratic leader specifically rely? His ability to

    A. listen and tactfully guide the discussion in the direction he has planned and the members' willingness to cooperate
    B. diagnose situations, to interpret and explain them to the members and their willingness to accept
    C. discern the issues which the members could profitably discuss and his willingness to allow them with his help to do so
    D. understand the meaning of the response from the member's frame of reference and his willingness for them to make decisions

19. Advisement in counseling is MOST effective when the counselee is in a state of

    A. perceiving his problem as related to a conflict with inner forces
    B. minimal conflict and of optimal readiness for action
    C. perceiving his problem as related to an external conflict
    D. feeling extremely ambivalent about his self-concept

20. Of the following, the MOST valid use of projective techniques is the study of the

    A. problems which an individual faces
    B. cultural effects upon an individual
    C. inner world of an individual
    D. human relationships of an individual

21. Diagnosis is NOT regarded as a helpful antecedent to counseling by 21.____

    A. Cottle   B. Rogers
    C. Thorne   D. Williamson

22. The beginning counselor must be alert to interferences to rapport. Which one of the following is NOT considered an intereference? 22.____

    A. Injecting the counselor's present mood
    B. Engaging in "small talk" at the start of the interview
    C. Registering surprise or dismay
    D. Emphasizing the counselor's ability

23. There is some evidence according to Rogers that counseling is more effective with 23.____

    A. younger adults or higher intelligence
    B. older adults of higher intelligence
    C. younger adults of lower intelligence
    D. older adults of lower intelligence

24. In assisting with the scheduling of interviews for educational planning, the counselor should suggest that group instruction 24.____

    A. follow the counseling interview
    B. is not necessary when individual interviews can be scheduled since each case is different
    C. precede the counseling
    D. may either precede or follow the counseling interview

25. A client has requested an interview with the counselor to discuss a personal problem. In general, the BEST way to begin the interview is to 25.____

    A. come directly to the point and encourage the client to talk about his problem
    B. assure him that everything discussed will be confidential
    C. offer to help him in every way possible
    D. inquire whether he has discussed the problem with anyone else

KEY (CORRECT ANSWERS)

1. C
2. A
3. C
4. B
5. D

6. A
7. B
8. C
9. B
10. C

11. A
12. B
13. B
14. A
15. D

16. C
17. A
18. C
19. B
20. C

21. B
22. B
23. A
24. C
25. A

EXAMINATION SECTION
TEST 1

DIRECTIONS: Each question or incomplete statement is followed by several suggested answers or completions. Select the one that BEST answers the question or completes the statement. *PRINT THE LETTER OF THE CORRECT ANSWER IN THE SPACE AT THE RIGHT.*

1. When a counselee describes a problem which is similar to one the counselor has had, the counselor usually should

    A. tell the counselee how he reacted in similar circumstances
    B. suggest solutions which worked for him
    C. describe his own experiences, but disguise them by saying they happened to another of his counselees
    D. make no reference to his experience

2. Of the following, the MOST highly specialized process in guidance is

    A. testing   B. occupational study
    C. interviewing   D. counseling

3. Which of the following is the MOST fundamental aim of guidance?

    A. Solve client's problems
    B. Counsel clients concerning problems
    C. Develop self-direction
    D. Direct the client to strive for excellence

4. A counselor forecasts the extent to which the counselee may or may not make a desirable or satisfying adaptation to his situation. Williamson referred to this step in the counseling process as

    A. synthesis   B. prognosis
    C. follow-up   D. diagnosis

5. A fundamental assumption made by the client-centered school of counseling is that

    A. diagnosis is essential to effective counseling
    B. every individual possesses a "tendency toward growth"
    C. responsibility for client actions is assumed by the counselor
    D. the counselor's role is primarily one of giving information to the counselee

6. Referral of a client to other agencies should be made

    A. after a long period of counseling has proved ineffectual
    B. only with the client's and his parent's consent
    C. as soon as the needed adjustment lies outside of client's, as well as counselor's, control
    D. after consultation with teachers and administration

7. According to field theory, individuals who are initially faced with a problem tend to seek

   A. long involved indirect solutions
   B. simple direct solutions
   C. outside help in forcing a solution
   D. means of withdrawing from the problem

8. In regard to client activity, the goal of counseling agreed upon by all methodologies is

   A. integrated controlled behavior
   B. release of feeling and negative emotion
   C. more individuals who understand themselves
   D. conformity to the cultural mores

9. A counselor who is primarily concerned with analyzing and diagnosing a client's problems, collecting and synthesizing data about the client, and making predictions about the consequences of various client decisions would BEST be classified as using which method of counseling? The

   A. *clinical* method as described by Williamson
   B. *client-centered* method as described by Rogers
   C. *communications* method as described by Robinson
   D. *learning* method as described by Dollard & Miller

10. Most definitions would NOT include which of the following as a necessary aspect of counseling?

    A. The counselor and client meet face-to-face.
    B. The client is experiencing a degree of emotional disturbance.
    C. A unique learning opportunity is provided for the client.
    D. The counselor brings special competence to the counseling relationship.

11. The *initial* counseling interview is considered by many to be hardest.
    Which one of the following is NOT an essential objective of this session? To

    A. develop a sound working relationship with the individual
    B. make a diagnosis of the client's problem
    C. orient the client to the nature of the counseling process
    D. provide an atmosphere that allows the individual to express freely his attitudes and feelings

12. A powerful dynamic in the counseling process and usually the very antithesis of its counterpart in the instructional process is

    A. encouraging accuracy
    B. emphasizing structure
    C. encouraging sequential orderly thinking
    D. processing ambiguity

13. Counseling techniques are useful in working with advantaged, bright or creative children. Fundamental is a counseling atmosphere that is

    A. non-threatening
    B. urging for creativity
    C. highly charged to stimulate excitement
    D. pretty well structured

14. Which one of the following counseling approaches emphasizes differential diagnosis in the treatment of individual clients?

    A. Trait- and factor-centered
    B. Self-theory
    C. Communications
    D. Psychoanalytic

15. The school of counseling theory, characterized by the attempt to observe behavior from the point of view of the individual himself (i.e., his own frame of reference), is known as

    A. organismic   B. neo-Freudianism
    C. existentialism   D. phenomenology

16. Of the following, which characteristic do counseling theorists consider MOST essential to the effectiveness of a counselor?

    A. Extroversion   B. Persuasiveness
    C. Serenity   D. Objectivity

17. The counseling approach which uses any of a variety of techniques which BEST suit individual situations is called

    A. instinctive   B. specific
    C. conditioning   D. eclectic

18. Mental testing, statistics, and measurement are identified *most closely* with which one of the following counseling approaches?

    A. Neobehavioral   B. Trait- and factor-centered
    C. Psychoanalytic   D. Communications

19. The "self-actualization" process is the central tendency of which one of the following approaches in counseling?

    A. Neobehavioral   B. Communications
    C. Self-theory   D. Psychoanalytic

20. In counseling, the LEAST acceptable introduction in phrasing an interpretative statement is which one of the following?

    A. "It seems as though..."
    B. "Do you suppose that..."
    C. "It probably would be better if..."
    D. "I'm wondering if..."

21. The term "ambiguity" in counseling refers to the degree of, openness or uncertainty that exists in the minds of both counselor and client regarding what is supposed to happen next.
    The ULTIMATE degree of ambiguity in counseling is represented by the use of

    A. open-ended leads
    B. depth interpretation
    C. "yes" and "no" questions
    D. free association

22. The client says, "I can't seem to get along with the other kids."
    Of the following, the MOST appropriate counselor response is:

    A. "Have you done your part?"
    B. "Let's talk about it."
    C. "You're too reserved and too cold."
    D. "You don't care very much about it."

23. In psychoanalytically-oriented counseling, the responsibility for the client's bringing up and talking about important material lies

    A. *exclusively* with the client
    B. *primarily* with the client, with the help of the counselor
    C. *primarily* with the counselor, with the cooperation of the client
    D. *exclusively* with the counselor

24. Research shows that, regardless of theoretical persuasion, experienced counselors as compared with less experienced counselors tend to

    A. use a wider range of techniques
    B. rely primarily on reflection of feeling
    C. use deeper interpretations
    D. take more responsibility for content

25. STRUCTURING in counseling is the process of

    A. building rapport in the initial interview
    B. establishing the ground rules for the counselor
    C. determining the client's real problem
    D. communicating and sharing expectations about counseling

KEY (CORRECT ANSWERS)

1. D
2. D
3. C
4. B
5. B

6. C
7. B
8. A
9. A
10. B

11. B
12. D
13. A
14. A
15. D

16. D
17. D
18. B
19. C
20. C

21. D
22. B
23. B
24. A
25. D

TEST 2

DIRECTIONS: Each question or incomplete statement is followed by several suggested answers or completions. Select the one that BEST answers the question or completes the statement. *PRINT THE LETTER OF THE CORRECT ANSWER IN THE SPACE AT THE RIGHT.*

1. Of non-white youngsters in the United States who drop out before completing 4 years of high school, what proportion come from families earning less than $20,000?

    A. 25%   B. 40%   C. Over 50%   D. Over 90%

2. Educational attainment has been rising. Median school years of attainment for persons now holding clerical or sales jobs average

    A. more than 12 years
    B. less than 12 years
    C. more than 10 years
    D. less than 10 years

3. From the client-centered point of view of counseling, information about the client's skills, personality, etc. are best used

    A. to help the counselor to understand the client better
    B. to help the client to understand himself better
    C. as a basis for the counselor's suggestions, which the client is free to reject
    D. as a part of the counselor's diagnosis in deciding how best to work with the client

4. Appropriate responses for a counselor include all of the following EXCEPT

    A. "If I were you..."
    B. "Can you tell me more about...?"
    C. "How do you feel about...?"
    D. "How long has this been going on...?"

5. During the early stages of a counseling relationship, a client engages in long periods of silence and appears to have difficulty in discussing questions which the counselor raises. A psychoanalytically-oriented counselor would *probably* interpret these silences and difficulties as signs of

    A. lack of rapport
    B. frustrated oral needs
    C. the client's inability to analyze his problems
    D. resistance to dealing with emotional problems

6. The single recent book which focuses specifically on problems of professionalization in counseling in the present society and makes dramatic recommendations for counselor training is THE COUNSELOR IN A CHANGING WORLD. The author is

    A. Dugald S. Arbuckle
    B. Edward C. Glanz
    C. Leslie E. Moser
    D. C. Gilbert Wrenn

7. All of above the following are identified with existential counseling EXCEPT

    A. Frankl
    B. May
    C. Van Kamm
    D. Eysenck

8. In the final analysis, realization of potential by the individual depends upon

   A. his abilities
   B. the limits imposed by his society and culture
   C. subjective interactional factors
   D. all of the above

9. Which one of the following is the MOST important deterrent to evaluation of guidance programs? Lack of

   A. objective data
   B. suitable criteria
   C. research skills among guidance workers
   D. data processing equipment

10. Acculturation, the process of acquiring values different from those of the culture into which one is born, can BEST be promoted through guidance of

    A. introducing the student to the new culture
    B. showing the student how the culture into which he was born is inadequate
    C. supporting the individual in learning the new culture and by rewarding him for the new learning
    D. showing the student that cultural differences are relatively unimportant

11. The client speaks so low that you cannot hear what he is saying.
    The BEST technique to use in handling this would be to

    A. confront the client with the problem
    B. pretend that you can hear him
    C. respond in like manner
    D. interpret this action to him as an "interpersonal defense mechanism"

12. All of the following are important in the "social-psychological" theories of counseling EXCEPT

    A. life style
    B. cognitive processes
    C. interpersonal relationships
    D. need for identity

13. In distinguishing between counseling and clinical psychology, which of the following tends to be TRUE of the counselor but not of the clinician?

    A. The major focus is on the normal, adaptive resources of the client's personality
    B. The use of psychological test data to contribute to a better understanding of the client
    C. A supportive and accepting relationship is developed
    D. The disintegrative, disturbed aspects of the client's personality receive major attention

14. Which of the following words is MOST similar in meaning to "reliability"?

    A. Consistency   B. Interpretability
    C. Objectivity   D. Truthfulness

15. Which of the following can be classified as an observational device?

    A. Anecdotal records
    B. Interest inventories
    C. Projective technique
    D. Personality inventories

16. As a guidance counselor, you may often be consulted by parents about how to respond more helpfully to teenagers. Which one of the following judgments about parent-teenager relationships is false?

    A. Parents' approval of work well done and pride in accomplishment means a great deal to the teenager, even though he brushes it off.
    B. For the sake of the young person's self-respect, it is a good idea to criticize him as much as possible.
    C. Giving a teenager opportunity for being in with a group is closely related to school progress.
    D. Parents' recognition and appreciation of good school progress, without putting on heavy pressure, is a help in keeping it up

17. In counseling, the term "understanding" refers to

    A. the counselor's ability to communicate how a client's behavior appears to other people
    B. the counselor's skill in grasping meanings the client's comments convey
    C. the counselor's adeptness in anticipating feelings of the client
    D. the counselor's knowledge of dynamics of personality

18. Of the following, the MOST significant difference between "psychotherapy" and "counseling" is in the

    A. goals and expected outcomes
    B. techniques used
    C. amount of psychological insight involved
    D. professional background of the counselor

19. Appropriate "bridges" for the counselor in counseling are all of the following EXCEPT

    A. "Let's move on to..."
    B. "We were talking about..."
    C. "What was it you said about...?"
    D. "How does this fit in with what you said earlier?"

20. From the client-centered point of view, "understanding" in counseling is BEST thought of as

    A. diagnosing the client's motivational structure
    B. seeing the client's world as he sees it
    C. following and accepting the client's spoken words
    D. the ability to predict future actions

21. The statement of a client MOST indicative of *transference* feelings is:

    A. "I really didn't feel like coming here today."
    B. "My mother doesn't approve of my talking to you."
    C. "If only you would tell me what I should do."
    D. "You remind me of my father."

22. In counseling, "reflection" refers to

    A. a restatement of the counselee's comment
    B. clarification of the content of the remark
    C. the counselor's perception of the feelings being expressed
    D. a non-committal statement such as "uh huh"

23. In the given paradigm, all are CORRECTLY matched EXCEPT:

	Counseling Model	Predominant Goal
A.	Psychoanalytic	insight
B.	Teacher-learner	sound decision and self-understanding
C.	Behavioral	shaping of specific responses
D.	Client-centered	catharsis

24. Freud believes that the client builds defenses against his inner conflicts when the therapeutic process tempts him to express conflictual impulses. These defenses result in resistance.
    According to Freud, such resistance in successful counseling

    A. is unavoidable
    B. is carefully avoided by the counselor
    C. indicates the counselor has proceeded too fast
    D. does not occur

25. Existential counseling includes all of the following characteristics EXCEPT

    A. a belief in universal values
    B. a subjective view of reality
    C. the total empathic response of the therapist
    D. the individual's intense awareness of his contingency and his freedom

KEY (CORRECT ANSWERS)

1. C
2. A
3. B
4. A
5. D

6. D
7. D
8. D
9. B
10. C

11. A
12. B
13. A
14. A
15. A

16. B
17. B
18. A
19. A
20. B

21. D
22. C
23. D
24. A
25. A

EXAMINATION SECTION
TEST 1

DIRECTIONS: Each question or incomplete statement is followed by several suggested answers or completions. Select the one that BEST answers the question or completes the statement. *PRINT THE LETTER OF THE CORRECT ANSWER IN THE SPACE AT THE RIGHT.*

1. Counselors adhering to the personality theory espoused by C.G. Jung often have to help people with problems related to what Jung called *individuation*.
   Jung defined this term as the process

   A. which occurs when adolescents leave home to establish their own residences
   B. occurring throughout life in which a person is becoming an individual
   C. through which parents come to have unique patterns of interaction with each of their children
   D. which is an outgrowth of the psychoanalytic principle of determinism

   1.____

2. A counselor completing a report for an insurance company was required to indicate whether a client had a phobia or an anxiety reaction.
   The counselor was able to indicate the correct classification because the counselor knew that the PRIMARY distinction between the two conditions is the

   A. age of onset of severe psychological distress
   B. ease with which the symptoms are eliminated
   C. frequency of symptom occurrence
   D. specificity of the fear-causing source

   2.____

3. Erikson presented an eight-stage theory of human development, the last stage of which he entitled Integrity versus Despair. A person's challenge in this stage is to achieve acceptance of the finality of life.
   Erikson postulated that such acceptance could be achieved *only* if the person had

   A. reached a parallel level of moral development
   B. established an economic environment such that the person need not be concerned about having good living conditions
   C. successfully met the challenges of the previous stages
   D. developed the ability to distinguish among the various roles the individual had filled in life

   3.____

4. Humanists in the existential tradition assert that personal decisions are (personally) effective only if they are made consistent with personal beliefs and principles, and regardless of whether they are in agreement with those of most people or the known consequences of the decisions.
   This assertion also is an appropriate description of which of Kohlberg's stages of moral development?

   A. Naively egotistic orientation
   B. Respect for authority and social order
   C. Contractual-legalistic orientation
   D. Conscience orientation

   4.____

5. A counselor was hired to develop educational activities that would promote development of gender-fair (i.e., non sex-role stereotypic) attitudes among older elementary-school-age children. The counselor decided to develop the activities within the context of social learning theory.
Which of the following activities would be MOST appropriate for use by the counselor?

   A. Having the children view movies that depict males in so-called traditionally feminine occupations (e.g., nursing) or activities (e.g., ironing) and vice versa
   B. Providing some reward (e.g., a small candy) to children who make gender-fair statements during a discussion of *what people do when they grow up*
   C. Instructing the children to ask their parents what their parents' beliefs are about appropriate roles for women and men
   D. Having the children share what they believe are each of their parent's feelings about activities they do (e.g., active and passive play behaviors)

6. In attempting to understand the life perspectives and characteristics of their clients, some counselors use Kohlberg's theory of moral development as a theoretical framework. These counselors know that Kohlberg's theory includes three progressive levels culminating in

   A. self-actualization, wherein the individual is fully humanistic
   B. principled thought, wherein the individual adopts a self-accepted set of standards of behavior
   C. androgyny, wherein the individual exhibits both male and female stereotypic behaviors
   D. personhood, wherein the individual is free from moral dilemmas

7. A professional counselor determines fees for monthly consultation services on a job-by-job basis.
This is an example of which of the following types of reinforcement schedules?

   A. Variable interval   B. Fixed interval
   C. Variable ratio   D. Fixed ratio

8. Competitiveness between children in the same family is known as

   A. sibling rivalry   B. the Oedipus conflict
   C. the Electra conflict   D. the Foundling conflict

9. A counselor in a social services agency working with economically deprived immigrants would focus on the person's most urgent need.
The FIRST priority would be the need for

   A. love   B. shelter and food
   C. friendship   D. education

10. The BEST descriptor of the emotion that results when a feeling of fear is not understood by the person experiencing it is

    A. anxiety   B. affect   C. anger   D. arousal

11. Many members of the counseling profession have engaged in social reform efforts intended to reduce spouse abuse.
    These efforts have had limited effect because

    A. spouse abuse occurs primarily among persons of low socioeconomic status, a group of people not generally prone to seek counseling services
    B. many people, both males and females, believe that spouse abuse is a *family matter* and, therefore, not subject to intervention from persons outside the family
    C. increasing incidence of incarceration of spouse abusers has reduced the need for counseling services
    D. all of the above

12. A counselor was working with a client who had been referred by a supervisor because the client had been having problems with co-workers, problems primarily attributable to the client's prejudicial attitudes toward ethnic minorities. The counselor asked how the client had come to hold the (prejudicial) attitudes the client was presenting. The client replied, *I don't really know or care. It just makes those folks easier to understand.*
    The client's statements reflect which of the following models that have been used to explain the formation of prejudicial attitudes?

    A. Social learning   B. Information processing
    C. Social conflict   D. Authoritarianism

13. A client was referred to a counselor by a physician. On the physician's advice, the client had been taking valium to alleviate *minor instances of stress.*
    Initially, small doses of valium were sufficient to alleviate the client's stress. However, over a period of approximately one year, the client had found it necessary to take increasingly larger doses to bring about similar stress reduction.
    The counselor surmised that the client had developed a(n) _____ reaction to the valium.

    A. psychological dependence
    B. addiction
    C. physical dependence
    D. tolerance

14. Because of the nature of the counseling process, some concepts from the field of speech and communications are readily applied to counseling. For example, counselors often find it appropriate to give (i.e., send) persuasive messages to clients. Such messages are more likely to be received (i.e., heard and accepted) if the counselor, as the message sender, exhibits certain characteristics.
    Which of the following is NOT a primary characteristic of effective persuasive communicators?

    A. Emotionality   B. Attractiveness
    C. Expertness   D. Trustworthiness

15. In recent years, the language used in federal and many state legislative acts relative to counseling services for persons with handicaps has tended to shift from the use of general categorical definitions to noncategorical definitions of functional limitations of handicapping conditions.
    This change appears to reflect a realization that

A. the medical (i.e., physical) diagnosis is the most accurate basis for determining an appropriate level of funding
B. a specific disability has essentially the same effect in any educational or work setting
C. funding bases should not incorporate considerations of categories of disabilities
D. all categorically disabled people do not have the same functional limitations in all work or education situations

16. Research on the development in a person of a so-called *humanistic life outlook* has shown that it is facilitated by

    A. formal educational experiences
    B. observational learning experiences
    C. diverse interpersonal interactions
    D. all of the above

17. When persons who are characteristically shy and withdrawn participate in *assertiveness training*, initially they experience uncertainty and self-doubt. Counselors refer to this social-psychological concept as

    A. cognitive dissonance
    B. dissociation
    C. individuation
    D. acculturation

18. A group of people living together with prescribed patterns of interdependent behavior could be BEST described as a

    A. culture   B. society   C. class   D. cult

19. Which of the following does NOT influence conformity to the expected standards of behavior within a culture?

    A. Physical punishment
    B. Praise
    C. Acceptance
    D. Events

20. In counseling older adults to achieve greater life satisfaction, counseling goals are more easily defined with the recognition that life satisfaction among older persons is PRIMARILY related to

    A. economic well-being
    B. sexuality
    C. self-concept
    D. all of the above

21. A counselor who follows an eclectic approach to counseling PRIMARILY bases the choice of utilized techniques upon

    A. the severity of the emotional distress exhibited by the client
    B. the client's intellectual, emotional, and environmental resources
    C. whether the client was referred or volunteered for counseling
    D. the theoretical orientation espoused in the counselor's professional preparation program

22. Client: *I just can't see myself working in a hospital, being around sick kids all day.*
    Counselor: *You just don't like kids.*
    The counselor in this example has made which of the following types of reflection error?

    A. Depth
    B. Capitulation
    C. Meaning
    D. Syntax

23. The counseling technique used by the counselor to explain to a client the logical inconsistencies in the client's statements is known as

    A. confrontation
    B. summarization
    C. paradoxical intention
    D. systematic desensitization

24. In the context of the reality therapy approach to counseling, the counselor strives to achieve a counseling relationship in which the counselor assumes a(n) _____ role in decision making relative to the client.

    A. superordinate   B. equal
    C. subordinate   D. antithetical

25. In Schein's *Doctor-Patient* model of consultation, which of the following conditions must be met for the consultation process to be effective?

    A. The consultee correctly interprets the symptoms identified.
    B. The consultee trusts that the consultant has provided accurate diagnostic information.
    C. The consultee is willing to implement the suggestions made by the consultant.
    D. All of the above conditions must be met.

26. A client comes to a counselor complaining of *being generally unhappy*. However, the client is unable to clarify further the nature of the unhappiness other than through vague allusions to being not interested in anything.
    At this point in the process, the counselor would be BEST advised to

    A. confront the client's inability to clarify the reasons for the unhappiness
    B. explore activities that the client enjoyed in the past
    C. use active-listening skills until the client is better able to describe the problem
    D. generate and discuss possible reasons for the client's unhappiness

27. Client: *Most of the time things are fine, but I hate it when my parents fight. It makes me want to run away from home.*
    Counselor: *Is it possible that you both love and hate your parents?*
    The counselor's response is an example of the counseling skill known as

    A. reflection   B. interpretation
    C. summarization   D. confrontation

28. Which of the following is a basic assumption underlying effective use of Caplan's Mental Health Consultation model?

    A. Mental health consultation is a supplement to other problem-solving mechanisms within an organization.
    B. Consultee attitudes and affect must be dealth with directly in the mental health consultation process.
    C. The technical expertise of the mental health consultant is sufficient for design of an effective intervention.
    D. The consultant and consultee share responsibility for case management.

29. Ellis' Rational Emotive Therapy and Meichenbaum's Cognitive Behavior Modification approaches to counseling are similar in that both hold that

    A. a client's cognitions are *hypotheses to be tested,* not absolute facts or truths
    B. clients should perform *personal experiments* to determine if cognitions and beliefs are consistent with objective reality
    C. *restructuring of cognitions* is an important aspect of therapeutic change
    D. all of the above

30. Clients and counselors sit closer together, presumably reflecting being psychologically closer, when they are similar in terms of factors such as age, social status, and general appearance (e.g., style of clothing worn).
    However, research in proxemics also has shown that forward (upper body) trunk lean by a counselor is likely to cause a negative, distancing reaction initially in a client who is

    A. depressed and crying
    B. less intelligent than the counselor
    C. a different race from the counselor
    D. much shorter than the counselor

31. Although group effectiveness is difficult to define and is related to the purposes and leadership of the group, some general principles have been agreed upon. For example, group processes generally are most effective when the group

    A. has an authoritarian leader who maintains interpersonal rules and directions for the group
    B. develops new ways of functioning in response to emerging needs and patterns of interaction among group members
    C. identifies group members who inhibit movement toward the group's goals
    D. works on several group tasks simultaneously, thereby increasing group efficiency

32. A counseling group member stated, *I feel so much better knowing that many of you have had similar problems. I guess we're all in the same boat!*
    This member's statement is an example of a group process phenomenon known as

    A. transference   B. universality
    C. catharsis   D. intellectualization

33. In some counseling groups the members feel dependent upon the group counselor (leader) for direction and movement and are passive in other ways as well, and the group counselor is easily fatigued and irritated because of the responsibility to *make everything work* in the group.
    According to Yalom (among others), this situation is MOST likely to arise in groups

    A. that have failed to establish self-disclosure as an appropriate behavior for group members
    B. in which unstructured, freely interactive behavior is the norm for group members
    C. in which the meaningfulness of the group to each of the respective members is too high
    D. that have not assumed responsibility for their own functioning

34. Which of the following is the LEAST important consideration that a group leader should employ in the selection of potentially appropriate strategies to be used in the group?

   A. The types of people who will constitute the group
   B. The leader's self-knowledge
   C. The members' previous experience in groups
   D. The extent to which the leader will be involved in the group

35. The members of a group seemed to be rebelling against the group counselor's leadership, *fighting* with one another to establish dominance in the group, confronting the group counselor as well as one another, and generally being in a state of conflict.
Based on these characteristics and behaviors, the group counselor determined that the group was in which of the following stages of group development?

   A. Orientation   B. Transition
   C. Action   D. Completion

36. Counselors know that groups are formed for different purposes. For example, in some groups the primary goal is to yield some specified outcome, or *product,* while in others the primary goal is to focus on the *process* of interaction within the group.
Which one of the following types of groups is more product than process oriented?

   A. Behavioral   B. Transactional-analysis
   C. Adlerian   D. Client-centered

37. In the context of group counseling, members who are high in conformity also tend to be high in

   A. independence   B. authoritarianism
   C. intelligence   D. superiority

38. Counselors refer to the study of *person-to-person relationships* within a group situation as

   A. syntaxicality   B. homeostatis
   C. sociometry   D. psychodrama

39. Which of the following is NOT a goal of Gestalt counseling groups?

   A. Helping individuals achieve integration
   B. Helping group members *grow up*
   C. Helping individuals accept anxiety as a part of life
   D. All of the above are Gestalt counseling goals

40. A specific technique for reinforcing desirable behaviors by pairing them with incompatible behaviors and incorporating principles of relaxation is

   A. satiation
   B. extinction gradient delineation
   C. mediation maximization
   D. systematic desensitization

KEY (CORRECT ANSWERS)

1. B	11. B	21. B	31. B
2. D	12. B	22. C	32. B
3. C	13. D	23. A	33. D
4. D	14. A	24. B	34. C
5. A	15. D	25. D	35. B
6. B	16. D	26. C	36. A
7. C	17. A	27. C	37. B
8. A	18. B	28. A	38. C
9. B	19. D	29. D	39. D
10. A	20. D	30. C	40. D

TEST 2

DIRECTIONS: Each question or incomplete statement is followed by several suggested answers or completions. Select the one that BEST answers the question or completes the statement. *PRINT THE LETTER OF THE CORRECT ANSWER IN THE SPACE AT THE RIGHT.*

1. At the conclusion of a year-long career counseling activity designed specifically for 34 *underemployed* persons, you are able to report to your supervisors that 22 of the participants changed to *training/education appropriate jobs,* 4 became unemployed, 5 remained in their same jobs, and 3 dropped out of the counseling program. This information is which of the following types of evaluation data?

   A. Process   B. Context   C. Product   D. Validity

   1.____

2. The *compensatory* theory of leisure suggests that a certified public accountant would enjoy _____, whereas the *spill-over* theory of leisure suggests that the accountant would enjoy _____ as a leisure activity.

   A. racquetball; chess
   B. backgammon; computerized games
   C. golf; tennis
   D. reading mysteries; bowling

   2.____

3. A counselor who works with adolescents is familiar with the knowledge that they tend to overselect professional positions and occupations when asked about *what they are planning to do for a living when they grow up.*
   In terms of Gelatt's decision-making paradigm, adolescents tend to have errors in their _____ systems.

   A. value   B. prediction
   C. generalization   D. decision

   3.____

4. A counselor who is following Super's theory of career development would not be surprised to learn that a person whom the counselor believed to be in the *Establishment* stage had

   A. quit work (altogether)
   B. changed jobs
   C. sought preretirement counseling
   D. been promoted to a management position

   4.____

5. One of the PRIMARY differences in clients' uses of career counseling resources in print media format (e.g., DICTIONARY OF OCCUPATIONAL TITLES or OCCUPATIONAL OUTLOOK HANDBOOK) and those in computerized format (e.g., CHOICES, DISCOVER II, SIGI, or ECES) is the

   A. number of jobs/occupations for which information is available
   B. speed with which information can be retrieved for use
   C. lack of need for counselors when the computerized format is used
   D. lack of need for the computerized format when the print media format is used

   5.____

6. A counselor who structures a career counseling group to help group members understand a *fields and levels* approach to careers is following the theory of

   A. Super B. Roe C. Holland D. Tiedeman

7. The concept of *career maturity* has been described and researched MOST extensively by

   A. Crites B. Hoyt C. Tiedeman D. Ginzberg

8. Which of the following is NOT one of the four major elements in Super's approach to career development?

   A. Vocational maturity
   B. Career patterns
   C. Values clarification
   D. Vocational life stages

9. The DICTIONARY OF OCCUPATIONAL TITLES

   A. would not be useful in face-to-face counseling with an individual
   B. is more useful than the OCCUPATIONAL OUTLOOK HANDBOOK
   C. could be useful in helping a counselee expand occupational options
   D. would be useful at the conclusion of the counseling process

10. Career counseling should include

    A. exploration of values and attitudes
    B. information and factual data about counselees, resources
    C. recognition of counselees' needs, conflicts, and relationships
    D. all of the above

11. A student obtained a score of 93 on a test having a standard error of measurement of 4 points.
    In interpreting the results, the counselor correctly informed the student that

    A. the student could not get a score above ninety-seven no matter how many times the test was retaken by the student
    B. the student had scored among the top eleven percent of those who had taken the test
    C. the student had achieved a score that was at least four points above the national mean
    D. more than likely the student would get a score between eighty-nine and ninety-seven if the student took the test again

12. In a consulting capacity with a local business college, a counselor had recommended administration of a clerical aptitude test to students in each of the two first-year classes; 35 students in one class and 29 students in the other. The tests had been scored by computer, and an internal consistency reliability coefficient of .78 had been found for the entire group. The counselor, however, was interested in the classes separately, and, therefore, calculated the reliability coefficients for each class.
    The counselor would expect the reliability coefficients for the separate classes to be _____ 78.

    A. lower than
    B. about the same as

C. higher than
D. insufficient information is provided to make an estimate

13. A counselor was reviewing pre-workshop *parenting knowledge* test data from a group of 40 couples (i.e., 80 respondents) who would soon be participating in a five-session workshop on parenting. The counselor observed that the local group's mean was essentially the same as the national mean but that there was a negative skew in the local group's test data.
The counselor correctly reported to the workshop participants that

  A. they, as a group, tended to be below average in parenting knowledge
  B. they, as a group, tended to be above average in parenting knowledge
  C. there was an error in scoring the test
  D. some participants could not benefit from participation in the workshop

13.____

14. A respondent took a standardized aptitude test which yielded percentile ranks for three normative groups. The respondent's results were as follows: 55th percentile for local norms, 69th percentile for state norms, and 61st percentile for national norms. A counselor interpreting these data could correctly conclude that

  A. similar respondent aptitude in the state is generally higher than local respondent aptitude
  B. similar respondent aptitude nationally is lower than respondent aptitude locally
  C. similar respondent aptitude nationally is lower than respondent aptitude in the state
  D. no valid comparisons among the respective distributions can be made from these data

14.____

15. In analyzing response data from a test, one type of information considered to be important in evaluating the test is the percentages of respondents who answered each item correctly.
This percentage is known as the item _____ index.

  A. discrimination   B. parameter
  C. proportionality   D. difficulty

15.____

16. Person A and Person B both took the same test. Person A got a score of 100 while Person B got a score of 75.
In order for a counselor to determine whether the difference between their scores was because of *chance,* the counselor would need to know which of the following characteristics of the test?

  A. Mean
  B. Standard deviation
  C. Standard error of measurement
  D. Standard error of the mean

16.____

17. A person got a score of 83 on a norm-referenced test. This means that the person

  A. mastered 83% of the material covered in the test
  B. achieved a score better than 83% of those taking the test
  C. answered 83 questions correctly
  D. sufficient information has not been provided to answer the question

17.____

18. A measure that is highly reliable can be depended on to

    A. be equivalent
    B. measure accurately
    C. give consistent results
    D. be specific

19. A client's _____ is a number that indicates how many persons taking the same test performed worse than or equal to the client.

    A. norm
    B. percentile rank
    C. rank equivalent
    D. test rank

20. If several raters report a high degree of agreement in assessing a person, their ratings could be characterized as having a high degree of

    A. validity
    B. identity
    C. discrimination
    D. reliability

21. A counselor is conducting a study wherein observers are rating frequency of aggressive behavior among a group of children in a play counseling group. Most of the children are neatly dressed and well groomed, but a very few are untidy and disheveled.
    If the observers' ratings are biased because they psychologically equate untidiness and aggressive behavior, it would be an example of the _____ effect in research.

    A. Hawthorne
    B. placebo
    C. multiple treatment
    D. halo

22. A standard deviation is a measure of

    A. discrepancy
    B. variability
    C. covariability
    D. stability

23. A counseling researcher computed a Pearson product-moment correlation coefficient of +.71 between the Graduate Record Examination Total (GRET) scores and the Graduate Grade-Point Averages (GGPA) of a group of 28 students in a counselor education program.
    The researcher correctly concluded that

    A. approximately half of whatever was being measured by GGPA also was being measured by GRET for that group of students
    B. the correlation coefficient was not statistically significant
    C. it would have been better to correlate separately the GRE Verbal and Quantitative subsection scores with GGPA
    D. a larger sample was needed to validly determine the correlation between the variables

24. A counseling researcher completed a study, the essence of which was that clients' ratings of counseling effectiveness were positively and statistically significantly related to counselors' frequencies of use of active listening (i.e., facilitative responding) skills. The counselor then wrote a manuscript describing the study and its results and implications, and submitted copies of it to the JOURNAL OF COUNSELING AND DEVELOPMENT, COUNSELOR EDUCATION AND SUPERVISION, and THE JOURNAL OF COUNSELING PSYCHOLOGY.
    The counselor was MOST likely to

    A. have the manuscript accepted for publication very soon

B. have the manuscript rejected because the findings were *old news* in the counseling profession
C. be advised to restructure the manuscript into a *brief report* format
D. be charged with violation of AACD's ethical standards and NBCC's code of ethics

25. A counseling researcher conducted a study in which adult males and females who had exhibited symptoms of depression were randomly assigned to one of three treatment conditions: (a) individual counseling, (b) group counseling, or (c) family counseling. For each condition, the counseling intervention was conducted for at least six weeks, at which time the Beck Depression Inventory was administered to the subjects. The researcher was particularly interested in *treatment x gender* interaction effects. Therefore, the researcher would be BEST advised to conduct a(n) _____ analysis of variance.

    A. one-way
    B. factorial
    C. multivariate
    D. bi-level

26. A counselor conducted a study intended to evaluate the effectiveness of ongoing group career counseling on the vocational maturity of high school sophomores. The study was begun in September and continued until June. This study is particularly susceptible to which of the following threats to the validity of an experiment?

    A. Regression
    B. Maturation
    C. Reactive effects of experimentation
    D. Multiple treatment interference

27. A counselor designs a study where two experimental groups and one control group complete pre- and post-experiment measures of self-concept. The subjects were not randomly assigned to the groups because of scheduling problems.
Which of the following techniques is MOST appropriate for analyzing the resultant data?

    A. Analysis of covariance
    B. Correlated t-tests
    C. Analysis of variance
    D. Wilcoxon matched-pairs signed-ranks test

28. If a theory covers a maximum of facts with a minimum of assumptions, it is referred to as being

    A. verifiable
    B. abstract
    C. concrete
    D. parsimonious

29. What would be the dependent variable in the statement *A rolling stone gathers no moss*?

    A. No
    B. Stone
    C. Moss
    D. Rolling

30. With which of the following types of experimental validity is the counseling researcher concerned when attempting to generalize research findings to other circumstances and subjects?

    A. Internal
    B. External
    C. Deductive
    D. Inductive

31. The Code of Ethics and the Ethical Standards of the American Association for Counseling and Development do NOT include a statement reflecting the principle that

   A. counselors have a right to protect clients from themselves if the clients give evidence of being self-injurious
   B. revelation of a counselor's notes on a client should not be made to other professionals unless the client has provided written permission to do so or the information has been subpoenaed by a court of law
   C. counselors should receive appropriate fees for services rendered regardless of the situations or settings in which the services were rendered
   D. improvement of the profession through a variety of professional involvements is a responsibility of all counselors

32. The state in which you reside does not yet have counselor licensure, so a local civic club has asked you to address their members to present an overview of counselor licensure and its benefits to the public.
In your presentation to the group, you note that

   A. licensure automatically entitles counselors to receive third-party payments from insurance companies
   B. some professional groups (e.g., psychologists) have opposed counselor licensure although the need for mental health services for the public has increased steadily
   C. state-level counselor licensure laws have existed for over twenty years although it is only recently that a majority of the states have counselor licensure laws
   D. one of the ways that counselor licensure laws protect the public's general welfare is through restriction of the use of the term *counselor* to those persons who have graduated from counselor education programs

33. A married couple comes to you, as a counselor in private practice, and tells you that they are having marital difficulties and have sought counseling for resolution of them. In the course of an initial session with them, one of the spouses reports being a new and active member of the local Alcoholics Anonymous (AA) group.
You should

   A. investigate the nature of the local AA's activities and continue counseling if those activities do not include accepted definitions of counseling
   B. terminate counseling with the one spouse but continue to work with the spouse who is not an AA participant
   C. offer to co-counsel with the staff of the local AA
   D. refer both spouses to the local AA

34. The Council for Accreditation of Counseling and Related Educational Programs (CACREP) STANDARDS FOR PREPARATION

   A. constitute the legal basis for certification and licensure requirements for professional counselors
   B. specify the minimum professional competencies (i.e., skills) which a counselor is expected to possess
   C. have been adopted by more than 60% of the approximately 480 counselor preparation programs in the United States
   D. are a set of guidelines for the desirable elements of and experiences in counselor preparation programs

35. A member of the local clergy telephones and asks for your evaluation of the moral values of a person whom the caller knows was one of your clients. The caller wants your opinion because the former client is an applicant to a theological institution for which the caller is the local applicant evaluator.
You should

   A. respond orally but require that no records be made of the conversation and that no comments be attributed to you
   B. inform the caller that under no circumstances are you ethically permitted to divulge the information requested
   C. inform the caller that you need to call the former client and obtain the client's permission before you can express your opinions
   D. seek the counsel of your supervisor to determine what types of information it would be permissible to divulge

36. You have been providing career counseling to a client who is seeking employment. Concurrent with the counseling, and with your knowledge, the client has made application for employment with several employers. A potential employer calls you and asks for your opinion as to your client's suitability for the employer's job opening.
Under which of the following conditions are you free (i.e., not in violation of professional ethics) to provide the information requested?

   A. When it is clear that the client will not get the job unless the information is given
   B. When you are certain that the information you would provide would assure that the client would get the job
   C. When in your best judgment you believe the information would enhance the client's chances for getting the job
   D. None of the above

37. As applied to professional licensure of counselors, the term *reciprocity* means that

   A. one licensing agency agrees to accept the licensing standards of another as sufficient for its own
   B. a licensed counselor may legally perform the functions of a licensed psychologist
   C. certification is synonymous with licensure
   D. graduation from a fully accredited counselor education program automatically constitutes eligibility for licensure

38. The publication that is likely to average the largest number of current research articles on the counseling process is the

   A. JOURNAL OF COUNSELING PSYCHOLOGY
   B. REVIEW OF EDUCATIONAL RESEARCH
   C. JOURNAL OF CONSULTING AND ABNORMAL PSYCHOLOGY
   D. JOURNAL OF NERVOUS AND MENTAL DISEASES

39. According to the Code of Ethics, when should a counselor try to persuade the client to report knowledge of a crime to the appropriate law enforcement authorities?

   A. When there is imminent danger to others
   B. When there is a crime in progress
   C. After the crime
   D. Never

40. Third-party reimbursement is a term pertinent to
    A. transactional analysis
    B. behavioral therapy
    C. insurance practices
    D. veterans' educational programs

KEY (CORRECT ANSWERS)

1. C	11. D	21. D	31. C
2. A	12. A	22. B	32. B
3. B	13. B	23. A	33. A
4. D	14. B	24. D	34. D
5. B	15. D	25. B	35. C
6. B	16. C	26. B	36. D
7. A	17. D	27. A	37. A
8. C	18. C	28. D	38. A
9. C	19. B	29. C	39. A
10. D	20. D	30. B	40. C

EXAMINATION SECTION
TEST 1

DIRECTIONS: Each question or incomplete statement is followed by several suggested answers or completions. Select the one that BEST answers the question or completes the statement. *PRINT THE LETTER OF THE CORRECT ANSWER IN THE SPACE AT THE RIGHT.*

1. A patient tells you that the other patients are plotting to kill him. This is MOST likely an example of

    A. a manic-depressive reaction
    B. a paranoid reaction
    C. excellent perceptual skills on the part of the patient
    D. a compulsive reaction

2. Which of the following statements is TRUE?

    A. Diagnoses are, by their very nature, always accurate.
    B. Phobic reactions are the most common reasons people are admitted to mental hospitals.
    C. People with neuroses are far less likely to be hospitalized than people with psychoses.
    D. Severely depressed patients are less of a suicide risk than any other patient group, except paranoid schizophrenics.

3. The LARGEST single diagnostic group of psychotic patients are

    A. neurotic depressive   B. schizophrenic
    C. obsessive-compulsive   D. paranoid reactive

4. The personality type that would BEST be characterized by the description that *he or she has no conscience* would be the

    A. drug addict   B. exhibitionist
    C. sociopath   D. manic-depressive

5. Of the following, the marked inability to organize one's thoughts is found MOST commonly and severely in

    A. schizophrenics
    B. amnesiacs
    C. those suffering from anxiety neuroses
    D. sociopaths

6. Someone who constantly feels tense, anxious, and worried but is unable to identify exactly why is MOST likely to be suffering from

    A. anxiety neurosis   B. schizophrenia
    C. dissociative reaction   D. a conversion reaction

7. A patient always insists upon twirling around six times before entering a new room, or she fears she will die. This is an example of

    A. paranoid reaction   B. obsessive-compulsive reaction
    C. dissociative reaction   D. anxiety neurosis

8. Of the following, those who suffer from neuroses would USUALLY complain of

   A. rejections, dissociation, and frequent inability to remember what day it is
   B. delusions, rejections, and feeling tired
   C. tiredness, fears, and hallucinations
   D. fears, physical complaints, and anxieties

9. The category that is caused by a disorder of the brain for which physical pathology can be demonstrated is

   A. neurotic depressive reaction
   B. schizophrenia
   C. functional psychoses
   D. organic psychoses

10. Of the following, which is NOT true?

    A. Someone who is suddenly unable to hear for psychological reasons would be considered to be suffering from a conversion reaction.
    B. If someone is in fugue, they have combined amnesia with flight.
    C. *Multiple personalities* is a dissociative reaction that affects primarily the elderly.
    D. General symptoms of schizophrenia include an ability to deal with reality, the presence of delusions or hallucinations, and inappropriate affect.

11. Which one of the following is TRUE?

    A. Calling an elderly person *gramps* or *granny* makes them feel more secure.
    B. It is important for an elderly person to maintain his or her independence whenever possible.
    C. When elderly patients start acting like children, they should be treated like children.
    D. It is important to encourage the elderly to hurry because they tend to move so slowly.

12. It has been found that older patients learn BEST when one does all but which one of the following?

    A. Allowing plenty of time for them to practice and learn
    B. Creating a relaxing environment for them
    C. Dealing with one thing at a time
    D. Assuming little knowledge on their part

13. Which of the following contains the main factors that should be considered before administering medications to elderly patients?

    A. How popular the medication is with the patient and the team leader's recommendations
    B. Any organic brain damage, liver dysfunction, and body weight
    C. Liver dysfunction, the patient's medical history, and decreased body weight
    D. Decreased body weight, impaired circulation, liver dysfunction, and increased sensitivity to medications

14. When communicating with the hearing impaired, it is BEST to do all of the following EXCEPT

    A. make sure the person can see your lips
    B. speak slowly and clearly
    C. use gestures
    D. shout

15. The three most common visual disorders in the elderly are cataracts, diabetic retinopathy, and glaucoma.
    Of the following statements about these, the one that is NOT true is that

    A. the symptoms for cataracts are a need for brighter light and a need to hold things very near the eyes
    B. diabetic retinopathy, if untreated, can cause blindness, so any vision or eye problems in diabetics should be promptly reported
    C. glaucoma develops slowly, so it is much easier to detect than cataracts or diabetic retinopathy
    D. some of the symptoms of glaucoma are loss of vision out of the corner of the eye, headaches, nausea, eye pain, tearing, blurred vision, and halos around objects of light

16. Which of the following is NOT true?

    A. Most of the elderly hospitalized for psychiatric problems suffer from senile brain atrophy or brain changes that occur due to arteriosclerosis.
    B. It is important to allow the elderly who wish to, the right to always live in the past.
    C. The majority of the elderly are competent, alert, and functioning well in their communities.
    D. Many elderly patients feel that they are no longer valued members of our society.

17. Of the following, which is NOT a good reason for helping the elderly patient stay active? Activity

    A. promotes good health by stimulating appetite and regulating bowel function
    B. prevents the complications of inactivity such as pneumonia, bed sores, and joint immobility
    C. can create an interest in taking more medication
    D. can increase blood circulation

18. Staff members must come to an understanding of their own feelings about the elderly because

    A. the staff may then be more helpful
    B. any negative feelings one has may be difficult to hide
    C. feelings of fear or aversion can be easily transmitted
    D. all of the above

19. An elderly patient will probably eat better if

   A. food servings are large
   B. the foods are chewy
   C. he or she is allowed to finish his/her meals at a leisurely pace
   D. cooked food is served cold

20. The MOST common accident to the elderly involves

   A. falls   B. burns   C. bruises   D. cuts

21. Which of the following is TRUE?

   A. Children should be considered and treated as miniature adults.
   B. Children are growing, developing human beings who will react to situations according to their level of development and the experiences to which they have been subjected.
   C. Children who are brought to a mental health center are usually calm and non-apprehensive on their first visit.
   D. The problems of adolescents are usually overestimated.

22. In working with adolescents, it would be BEST to

   A. neither bend over backwards to give in to demands, nor control them by rigid and punitive means
   B. dress the way most adolescents do
   C. staff those units with young people
   D. watch television with them regularly

23. Of the following, when working with children, it is MOST important to be

   A. consistent
   B. strict
   C. more concerned for their welfare than for the welfare of the other patients
   D. well-liked

24. Of the following, the element that is MOST lacking in relationships between adolescents and adults is

   A. respect   B. fear   C. trust   D. sensitivity

25. Of the following, the BEST reason for grouping children together would be

   A. they should be protected from the influences of all adult patients
   B. children tend to feel more comfortable with other children
   C. children are less likely to *act out* when they are with other children
   D. they would be unable to bother adult patients

26. All of the following statements are true EXCEPT:

    A. Accidents, reactions to drugs, fevers, and disease may each contribute to mental or emotional problems
    B. How effectively an individual reacts to and manages stress contributes to his or her mental health
    C. There is significant research that indicates that mental illness is caused primarily by genetic transmittal
    D. A person's upbringing, his or her relationships with family or friends, past experiences, and present living conditions may all contribute to the status of his or her mental health

27. All of the following are basic psychological needs which must be met for a person to have self-esteem EXCEPT

    A. acceptance and understanding
    B. trust, respect, and security
    C. a rewarding romantic relationship
    D. pleasant interactions with other people

28. All of the following statements are true EXCEPT:

    A. Most people become mentally ill because they are unable to cope with or adapt to the stresses and problems of life
    B. People with emotional problems can rarely be helped enough to live independently
    C. Most of the diseases and symptoms of the body which plague people have a large emotional component as their cause
    D. Environmental and familial factors are more important than genetic factors in mental illness

29. The following are all optimal aspects of family functioning EXCEPT

    A. communication is open and direct
    B. expression of emotion is more often positive than negative
    C. minor problems are ignored, knowing they will go away on their own
    D. there is a high degree of congruence or harmony between the family's values and the actual realities of the society

30. All of the following statements are true EXCEPT:

    A. People who are wealthy rarely become mentally ill
    B. Physical disease may influence emotional balance
    C. People who are mentally ill are often very sensitive to what is happening in their environment
    D. Most people doubt their own sanity at one time or another

31. All of the following statements are true EXCEPT:

    A. Hereditary factors are not the primary cause of mental illness
    B. A person may react to an extremely traumatic experience by becoming mentally ill
    C. Early recognition and treatment does not affect the course of mental illness
    D. Mental illness can develop suddenly

32. All of the following statements are true EXCEPT:

    A. Emotionally disturbed people are usually very sensitive to how other people feel towards them
    B. People do not inherit mental disorders, but may inherit a predisposition to certain types of mental problems
    C. There are many factors which can cause mental illness
    D. Mood swings are signs of mental illness

33. Which of the following statements is LEAST accurate?

    A. The difference between being mentally healthy and mentally ill often lies in the intensity and frequency of inappropriate behavior.
    B. The way a person views a situation determines his or her response to the situation.
    C. The mentally ill are permanently disabled.
    D. Different personal experiences cause a difference in what a person perceives as stressful, and how much stress a person can tolerate.

34. All of the following statements are true EXCEPT:

    A. Most experts in the field of mental health believe that the experiences which occur during the first twenty, or the first six, years of life are the most significant
    B. An unfortunate characteristic of children is that they tend to blame themselves for failures of their parents, and thus may develop feelings of inadequacy which may affect them all of their lives
    C. If neglect is severe enough, an infant or young child may withdraw from reality into a fantasy world which feels less threatening
    D. Human beings develop in the exact same pattern and almost at the same rate

35. Schizophrenia is

    A. genetically caused
    B. most often caused by the habitual use of drugs
    C. the result of a complex relationship between biological, psychological, and sociological factors
    D. most commonly caused by the inhalation of toxic gases

KEY (CORRECT ANSWERS)

1.	B	16.	B
2.	C	17.	C
3.	B	18.	D
4.	C	19.	C
5.	A	20.	A
6.	A	21.	B
7.	B	22.	A
8.	D	23.	A
9.	D	24.	C
10.	C	25.	B
11.	B	26.	C
12.	D	27.	C
13.	D	28.	B
14.	D	29.	C
15.	C	30.	A

31. C
32. D
33. C
34. D
35. C

TEST 2

DIRECTIONS: Each question or incomplete statement is followed by several suggested answers or completions. Select the one that BEST answers the question or completes the statement. *PRINT THE LETTER OF THE CORRECT ANSWER IN THE SPACE AT THE RIGHT.*

1. Tardive dyskenesia is a(n)

    A. antidepressant
    B. birth-related serious injury
    C. serious side effect of phenothiazine derivatives
    D. antiparkinsons drug

2. People taking psychotropic drugs are MOST likely to be sensitive to

    A. long exposures to sunlight
    B. darkness
    C. noise
    D. other patients

3. An antipsychotic drug that is a phenothiazine derivative would MOST likely be used for

    A. helping a patient lose weight
    B. calming a patient
    C. helping a patient sleep
    D. reducing the frequency of delusions in a patient

4. Of the following, an antidepressant such as Elavil would MOST likely be used for

    A. the immediate prevention of suicidal action in a newly admitted patient
    B. helping a patient lose weight
    C. elevating a patient's mood
    D. diuretic purposes

5. Which of the following statements is NOT true?

    A. Antianxiety tranquilizers such as sparine, librium, and vistaril are useful primarily with psychoneurotic and psychosomatic disorders.
    B. Minor or antianxiety tranquilizers tend to be less habit-forming than major or antipsychotic tranquilizers.
    C. Akinesia, pseudoparkinsonism, and tardive dyskenesia are serious side effects of antipsychotic drugs, or phenothiazine derivatives.
    D. Generally, those using tranquilizers like sparine or librium are in less danger of deadly drug overdoses than those using barbituates.

6. All of the following statements are false EXCEPT:

    A. Antipsychotic drugs promote increased sexual interest
    B. Patients no longer need to take their medication when they feel better
    C. Phenothiazines are psychotropic drugs
    D. One of the main difficulties with antipsychotic drugs is that they tend to be habit-forming

7. Yellowing of the skin or eyes, sensitivity to light and pseudoparkinsonism may occur in patients receiving   7.____

   A. mellaril or thorazine
   B. librium or tranxene
   C. valium or vistaril
   D. antiparkinson drugs

8. Which of the following is NOT true of extrapyramidal symptoms (EPS)? They   8.____

   A. may appear after many weeks of use of phenothiazines
   B. can safely be controlled without medical assistance
   C. may appear after the patient has been taking the drug for only a few days
   D. may include pseudoparkinsonism

9. The time required to reach an effective blood level for an antidepressant medication would MOST likely be three   9.____

   A. days   B. hours   C. weeks   D. months

10. An example of a psychotropic drug would be   10.____

    A. seconal   B. aspirin   C. librium   D. perichloz

11. In evaluating a patient you are meeting for the first time, it would be best NOT to   11.____

    A. be as objective as possible
    B. question one's own motives and reactions when processing data during and after the meeting
    C. be extremely goal-oriented
    D. not allow any praise or criticism directed at you by the patient to influence your assessment

12. All of the following statements are true EXCEPT: 12.____

    A. People communicate non-verbally via their behavior and their body posture
    B. Non-verbal clues may be a better indication of a patient's true feelings than what the patient actually says
    C. A patient who is highly anxious is easier to evaluate than a patient who is relatively calm
    D. People should be judged objectively

13. When asking a patient a question, one should do all of the following EXCEPT   13.____

    A. phrase questions in order to receive a yes or no response
    B. ask only relevant questions
    C. listen carefully to the response before asking the next question
    D. phrase questions clearly

14. The MAIN purpose for extensive record keeping is to   14.____

    A. provide an accurate description of the patient's diagnosis
    B. provide a subjective report of the patient's behavior
    C. provide an objective report of the patient's behavior
    D. give mental health personnel something to do

15. When talking to a patient for the first time, one must realize that

    A. hostile behavior indicates an extremely severe disorder in the patient
    B. a patient's physical appearance will indicate how successful you will be in communicating with the patient
    C. the patient is extremely nervous
    D. you are both strangers to each other

16. Of the following, which statement is NOT true?

    A. The rapid assessment of a patient is not necessarily accomplished by asking a series of routine questions.
    B. There is value, in assessing a patient, in creating a conversational bridge which has *here and now* relevance.
    C. One can assess a patient's state by his or her reaction to a warm greeting given to him or her.
    D. There is some value in routinely asking certain questions, when needed, in order to check a patient's orientation and memory.

17. All of the following could be signs that someone is moving towards mental illness EXCEPT

    A. exhibiting a degree of prolonged, constant anxiety, apprehension, or fear which is out of proportion with reality
    B. severe appetite disturbances
    C. occasional depression
    D. abrupt changes in a person's behavior

18. The first few minutes of interaction with a patient can reveal all but

    A. a patient's contact with reality
    B. whether you are comfortable with a patient
    C. a patient's mood
    D. a patient's chances for recovery

19. Which of the following statements is TRUE?

    A. The tentative diagnosis made when a patient is first admitted is the most accurate diagnosis.
    B. One should always try and keep in mind the state the patient was in when first admitted.
    C. A diagnosis is actually an ongoing process.
    D. When assessing patients' behavior, it is best to be suspicious of what may look like progress.

20. All of the following are examples of defense mechanisms EXCEPT

    A. projection
    B. complimenting someone
    C. displacement
    D. regression

21. A treatment plan is likely to be MOST effective if the

    A. patient's suggestions are always incorporated
    B. patient is voluntarily and wholeheartedly participating in the treatment plan designed for him or her

C. patient has daily contact with his or her family
D. patient respects the team leader

22. All of the following are true EXCEPT:

    A. Patients do not become well simply by people doing something for them
    B. A patient's well-being is enhanced when one or more team members can forge a *therapeutic alliance* with that patient
    C. The most important purpose of the treatment team is to administer the proper medications to patients
    D. It is important that a patient be seen as an individual, and not just as a *case* or a *number*

23. Of the following, a member of the treatment team can BEST assist a patient by

    A. commanding respect from other team members
    B. carefully observing the behavior of patients
    C. avoiding spending too much time with patients
    D. becoming friends with a patient

24. Of the following, which is LEAST important when considering a treatment plan?

    A. Involving the patient
    B. Setting reasonable goals
    C. Being as specific as possible in setting completion dates for goals, and sticking to them
    D. Detailing the methods to be followed, and the work assignments

25. All of the following are true EXCEPT:

    A. A treatment team should help patients understand that they can improve their condition if they will cooperate with the treatment plan
    B. Patients should be encouraged to participate in the programs designed for them
    C. Patients should be encouraged to revise their treatment plans
    D. One's approach should be tailored for each individual, whenever possible

26. All of the following could be considered appropriate goals for patients to work towards, EXCEPT to

    A. expand one's capacity to find or create acceptable options
    B. learn to be less dependent
    C. give up feeling persecuted
    D. learn how to get what one needs, at any cost

27. In working in treatment teams, it is MOST important for team members to

    A. communicate effectively with each other
    B. enjoy working with each other
    C. keep morale high
    D. attend meetings on time

28. One of the purposes of the treatment team is to

    A. decrease the amount of work
    B. coordinate and integrate services to patients
    C. provide training
    D. provide patients with basic counseling skills they can use

29. When working with someone exhibiting a manic-depressive psychosis, depressed type, it is BEST to

    A. concern yourself primarily with his or her eating habits
    B. focus primarily on their sleeping habits
    C. take every statement he or she may make about suicide seriously
    D. allow them to watch a great deal of television

30. In working with a paranoid patient, all of the following are true EXCEPT:
    It

    A. is important to listen with respect
    B. is helpful to establish a trusting relationship
    C. is good to try and talk the patient out of his or her fears
    D. would not be a good practice to agree with their statements, if they are not true

31. It is important, when dealing with verbally abusive patients, to keep in mind all of the following EXCEPT:

    A. Patients usually become abusive because of frustrating circumstances beyond their control
    B. In most cases, the patients do not mean anything personal by their abusive remarks; they are displacing anger
    C. It is important for staff members to remain calm and controlled when patients have emotional outbursts
    D. It is a good idea to allow an angry patient to draw you into an argument, as this will eventually help calm him or her down

32. When dealing with a patient who insists upon doing a number of rituals before brushing his teeth, it would be BEST to

    A. attempt to tease him out of his behavior
    B. not be critical of the ritualistic behavior
    C. perform the same rituals so that he feels more secure
    D. insist that he eliminate one step of the ritual each week

33. A patient tells you that he is balancing an automobile on the top of his head, and asks you what you think of that.
    An APPROPRIATE response for you to make would be:

    A. to ask him to take you for a ride
    B. *Stop saying ridiculous things*
    C. *I know you believe you are balancing a car on your head but I don't see it, therefore I have to assume that you're not*
    D. *Is it an invisible car*

34. A new patient, who is very paranoid, refuses to take off his clothes before getting into bed.
Which would be MOST helpful?

   A. Getting another staff member to assist in removing his clothes
   B. Leaving the room until he comes to his senses
   C. Trying to find out why the patient does not want to undress
   D. Allowing the patient to stay up all night

35. In handling depressed patients, it is BEST to

   A. encourage them to participate in activities
   B. remind them often that things will be better tomorrow
   C. remember that depressed patients have few feelings of guilt
   D. let them know that you know just how they are feeling

36. A patient tells you that she is very depressed over the recent death of her brother.
Which of the following would be the MOST appropriate response?

   A. *Everybody gets depressed when they lose someone they love.*
   B. *It could have been worse; at least he was ill only a short time.*
   C. *I know just how you feel.*
   D. *This must be very difficult for you.*

37. A patient who recently suffered a stroke refuses to let you help her bathe.
This is probably because

   A. it is hard for her to accept that she can no longer do things for herself that she could do before the stroke
   B. she does not like you
   C. she is extremely independent and should be encouraged to be less so
   D. you need to review your methods for bathing patients

38. All of the following would be appropriate in working with a patient who is hallucinating EXCEPT

   A. carefully watch what you are non-verbally communicating
   B. ask concrete, reality-oriented questions
   C. provide a calm, structured environment
   D. agree with the patient, if asked, that you are experiencing the same state he or she is

39. In dealing with overactive patients, it is BEST to

   A. not give most of your attention to these patients, leaving the quieter patients to look after themselves
   B. keep in mind that overactive patients are always more interesting than other patients
   C. remember that overactive patients need more care than other patients
   D. forcibly restrain them whenever possible

40. A patient with mild organic brain damage is very withdrawn and negativistic. The BEST approach, of the following, would be

    A. *I need a partner to play cards with me*
    B. *Your family is **very** disappointed in you when you act like this*
    C. *Your doctor said you should participate in all activities here, so you'd better do that*
    D. *Would you like to go to your room so you can be alone?*

40.____

KEY (CORRECT ANSWERS)

1. C	11. C	21. B	31. D
2. A	12. C	22. C	32. B
3. D	13. A	23. B	33. C
4. C	14. C	24. C	34. C
5. B	15. D	25. C	35. A
6. C	16. C	26. D	36. D
7. A	17. C	27. A	37. A
8. B	18. D	28. B	38. D
9. C	19. C	29. C	39. A
10. C	20. B	30. C	40. A

EXAMINATION SECTION
TEST 1

DIRECTIONS: Each question or incomplete statement is followed by several suggested answers or completions. Select the one that BEST answers the question or completes the statement. *PRINT THE LETTER OF THE CORRECT ANSWER IN THE SPACE AT THE RIGHT.*

1. Which of the following findings is MOST consistent with early alcohol withdrawal?
   A. Heart rate of 50-60 beats per minute
   B. Heart rate of 120-140 beats per minute
   C. Blood pressure of 90/60 mmHg
   D. Blood pressure of 140/80 mmHg

1.____

2. Which of the following patients would have the HIGHEST risk for suicide?
   A. Patient who talks about wanting to die
   B. Patient who plans a violent death and has the means to do so
   C. Patient who appears depressed, frequently thinks about dying, and gives away all personal possessions
   D. Patient who says they may do something if life does not improve soon

2.____

3. Which medical condition is commonly associated with patients with bulimia nervosa?
   A. Diabetes   B. HIV   C. Cancer   D. Hepatitis C

3.____

4. What action would be considered as a primary nursing intervention for a victim of child abuse?
   A. Teach the victim coping skills
   B. Ensure the safety of the victim
   C. Analyze the family dynamics
   D. Assess the scope of the problem

4.____

5. Somatoform disorder is defined as
   A. management consisting of a specific medical treatment
   B. expression of conflicts through bodily symptoms
   C. a voluntary expression of psychological conflicts
   D. physical symptoms explained by organic causes

5.____

6. What is a proper plan for treating a school-age child with attention deficit hyperactivity disorder?
   A. Ignore the child's hyperactivity
   B. Child should be removed from the classroom when disruptive
   C. Child should have as much structure as possible
   D. Encourage the child to play to release excess energy

6.____

7. Which characteristic is common for a child with conduct disorder?
   A. Ritualistic behaviors
   B. Preference for inanimate objects
   C. Severe violations of age-related normal behavior
   D. Easily distracted

8. School phobia is commonly relieved by
   A. allowing the parent to be with the child in the classroom
   B. immediately returning the child to school with a family member
   C. telling the student why attendance at school is important
   D. allowing the child to enter the school before the other children

9. If a child has an I.Q. of 45, what classification of mental retardation does this value represent?
   A. Mild   B. Moderate   C. Severe   D. Profound

10. Which characteristics are common for a child with autistic disorder?
    A. Aggression, stealing, lying
    B. Easily distracted, impulsive, and hyperactive
    C. Intolerant to change, disturbed relatedness, stereotypes
    D. Angry, argumentative, and disobedient

11. Which of the following would NOT be an acceptable therapeutic approach for caring for an autistic child?
    A. Providing safety measures
    B. Rearranging the environment to motivate the child
    C. Engaging a diversion when acting out
    D. Providing an atmosphere of acceptance

12. According to Piaget's Cognitive Stages of Development, a 5-year-old child is in what stage of development?
    A. Sensorimotor stage
    B. Concrete operations
    C. Pre-operational
    D. Formal operation

13. What is indicated if a patient states they have to increase their level of alcohol intake to achieve the desired effect?
    A. Tolerance
    B. Withdrawal
    C. Intoxication
    D. Weight gain

14. If an alcoholic patient is experiencing tremors, irritability, hypertension, and fever, what condition will soon follow?
    A. Esophageal varices
    B. Korsakoff's syndrome
    C. Wernicke's syndrome
    D. Delirium tremens

15. What would be the proper treatment for a patient in delirium tremens?
    A. Adequate fluids and high nutrient foods
    B. Placed in a quiet, dimly lit room
    C. Administration of Librium
    D. Monitoring vital signs every hour

16. If a patient presents with hallucinations, agitation, and an irritated nasal septum, which illicit drug did the patient MOST likely ingest?
    A. Marijuana
    B. Cocaine
    C. Heroin
    D. Methamphetamine

16.____

17. What would be the appropriate medication for a patient who presents with needle tracks in the arm, in a stupor, and with a pinpoint pupil?
    A. Narcan
    B. Methadone
    C. Naltrexone
    D. Disulfiram

17.____

18. If an elderly patient presents with increasing forgetfulness, decreasing daily function, and using a toothbrush to comb his hair, which of the following conditions is being exhibited by this patient?
    A. Aphasia
    B. Amnesia
    C. Apraxia
    D. Agnosia

18.____

19. What would be a PRIMARY treatment intervention for a patient with moderate stage dementia?
    A. Providing a safe and secure environment
    B. Providing adequate nutrition and hydration
    C. Encouraging memories to decrease isolation
    D. Encouraging to independently care for themselves

19.____

20. Through which characteristic is dementia different from delirium?
    A. Dementia promotes slurred speech
    B. Dementia has a gradual onset
    C. Dementia includes clouding of the consciousness
    D. Dementia includes a sensory perceptual change

20.____

21. What would be the BEST advice you could give to a patient who feels the need to starve themselves?
    A. Exercise until the need to starve passes
    B. Allow the patient to starve to relieve anxiety
    C. Tell the patient's family immediately
    D. Tell the patient to approach a nurse and talk out their feelings

21.____

22. Which characteristic is a sign of improvement for patients with anorexia nervosa?
    A. Weight loss
    B. Weight gain
    C. Eating meals in the dining room
    D. Participation in group activities

22.____

23. What is the MAJOR difference between anorexia nervosa and bulimia nervosa?
    Bulimic patients
    A. will have periods of binge eating and purging
    B. will have lesser anxiety
    C. will have peculiar food handling patterns
    D. have poor self-esteem

23.____

24. A caregiver can build a therapeutic relationship with a bulimic patient by performing all of the following actions EXCEPT
    A. discussing their eating behavior
    B. establishing an atmosphere of trust
    C. helping patients identify feelings associated with binging and purging
    D. educating the patient about the condition of bulimia nervosa

25. Which condition would be characterized by an intense fear of riding in an elevator?
    A. Arachnophobia
    B. Agoraphobia
    C. Xenophobia
    D. Claustrophobia

KEY (CORRECT ANSWERS)

1.	B	11.	B
2.	B	12.	C
3.	A	13.	A
4.	C	14.	D
5.	B	15.	D
6.	C	16.	B
7.	C	17.	A
8.	B	18.	D
9.	B	19.	A
10.	C	20.	B

21.	D
22.	B
23.	A
24.	A
25.	D

TEST 2

DIRECTIONS: Each question or incomplete statement is followed by several suggested answers or completions. Select the one that BEST answers the question or completes the statement. *PRINT THE LETTER OF THE CORRECT ANSWER IN THE SPACE AT THE RIGHT.*

1. What should be the INITIAL treatment action for a patient with claustrophobia?
    A. Accept the patient's fear without opinion or criticism
    B. Assist the patient to find the cause of the fear
    C. Allow the patient to talk about their fear as much as possible
    D. Establish a trusting relationship

    1.____

2. Which is evidence of a caregiver developing a countertransference reaction?
    A. Confronting the patient about discrepancies in their behavior
    B. Revealing personal information to the patient
    C. Focusing on the feelings of the patient
    D. Ignoring the patient's wants and needs

    2.____

3. In attempting to be accomplished when conducting desensitization, the patient
    A. stops using illicit drugs
    B. stops abusing alcohol
    C. overcomes disabling fear
    D. admits to all wrongdoings

    3.____

4. Which of the following should you advise patients who are prescribed to take valium?
    A. Increase fluid intake
    B. Decrease fluid intake
    C. Avoid caffeinated beverages
    D. Avoid alcoholic beverages

    4.____

5. How does malingering differ from somatoform disorder?
    A. Malingering is stress that is expressed through physical symptoms
    B. Malingering is gratification from the environment
    C. Malingering has evidence from an organic basis
    D. Malingering is a deliberate effort to handle upsetting events

    5.____

6. What is the MOST successful form of therapy for a somatoform disorder?
    A. Prescription medications
    B. Stress management
    C. Psychotherapy
    D. Milieu therapy

    6.____

7. What method would you use to treat a psychiatric patient who speaks a foreign language?
    A. Use pictures to communicate
    B. Speak in universal phrases
    C. Simply use nonverbal communication
    D. Employ the services of an interpreter

    7.____

8. The _____ theory attempts to explain obsessive compulsive behaviors related to unconscious conflicts between id impulses and the superego.
   A. cognitive
   B. psychoanalytic
   C. behavioral
   D. interpersonal

9. _____ the patient's obsessive compulsive disorder is the MOST successful behavior when caring for a patient with obsessive-compulsive disorder?
   A. Rejecting   B. Preventing   C. Accepting   D. Challenging

10. Which of the following characteristics would NOT be a factor for a patient having diminished sexual arousal?
    A. Medications
    B. Health status
    C. Education and work history
    D. Relationship with spouse

11. Getting the patient to _____ is the ultimate goal of treating a patient with somatoform disorder.
    A. take the prescribed medications
    B. recognize the signs and symptoms of physical illness
    C. cope with physical illness
    D. express anxiety verbally rather than through physical symptoms

12. What is MOST important when counseling a family whose teenage son has just been diagnosed with schizophrenia?
    A. The distressing symptoms of schizophrenia can respond to medications.
    B. Symptoms of this disease imbalance the brain.
    C. Genetic history is a factor for developing schizophrenia.
    D. Schizophrenia can affect every aspect of a patient's functioning.

13. A patient who states they only abuse alcohol and cocaine to deal with a stressful marriage and stressful job is exhibiting which defense mechanism?
    A. Displacement
    B. Rationalization
    C. Sublimation
    D. Projection

14. A pregnant female continues to use heroin throughout her pregnancy. Which of the following conditions would this child be at risk for developing?
    A. Heroin dependence
    B. Mental retardation
    C. Schizophrenia
    D. Anorexia nervosa

15. What is the MOST important medical intervention when caring for a victim of sexual assault?
    A. Preserving an unbroken chain of evidence
    B. Preserving the patient's privacy
    C. Determining the identity of the attacker
    D. Assessing for sexually transmitted diseases

16. Which of the following is NOT a factor for a victim of family violence to safely remain in the home?
    A. Ability of patient to relocate
    B. Socioeconomic status of the family
    C. Availability of community shelters
    D. A non-abusive family member to intervene on behalf of the victim

16.____

17. Inability to _____ would be a sign of early onset of Alzheimer's disease.
    A. balance a checkbook
    B. take care of self
    C. relate to family members
    D. remember own name

17.____

18. Which neurotransmitter is responsible for the development of Alzheimer's disease?
    A. Serotonin
    B. Dopamine
    C. Epinephrine
    D. Acetylcholine

18.____

19. What products should be avoided by patients who are taking lithium carbonate to stabilize moods?
    A. Caffeine   B. Diuretics   C. Antacids   D. Antibiotics

19.____

20. Which of the following situations would NOT increase stress on a healthy family system?
    A. Birth of a child
    B. Parental arguments
    C. Child going away to college
    D. Death of a grandparent

20.____

21. Patients who take monoamine oxidase inhibitors as antidepressants should avoid
    A. dairy and green vegetables
    B. red meat and poultry
    C. aged cheese and red wine
    D. flour, grains, and rice

21.____

22. What should a caregiver assess prior to administering thorazine to an agitated patient?
    A. Pulse rate
    B. Blood pressure
    C. Blood urea nitrogen level
    D. Liver enzymes

22.____

23. A patient who is prescribed benzodiazepine oxazepam should avoid excessive consumption of
    A. shellfish   B. coffee   C. sugar   D. salt

23.____

24. What is the PRIMARY purpose of Alcoholics Anonymous?
    A. Teach positive coping mechanisms
    B. Alleviate stress
    C. Help members maintain sobriety
    D. Provide fellowship among members

24.____

25. What would be the initial treatment intervention if a patient experiences a panic attack in your presence? 25.____
 A. Remain with patient and promote a safe environment
 B. Reduce external stimuli
 C. Encourage physical activity
 D. Teach coping mechanisms

KEY (CORRECT ANSWERS)

1. A
2. B
3. C
4. D
5. D

6. B
7. D
8. B
9. C
10. C

11. D
12. A
13. B
14. A
15. A

16. B
17. A
18. D
19. B
20. B

21. C
22. B
23. B
24. C
25. A

PREPARING WRITTEN MATERIAL

PARAGRAPH REARRANGEMENT
COMMENTARY

The sentences that follow are in scrambled order. You are to rearrange them in proper order and indicate the letter choice containing the correct answer at the space at the right.

Each group of sentences in this section is actually a paragraph presented in scrambled order. Each sentence in the group has a place in that paragraph; no sentence is to be left out. You are to read each group of sentences and decide upon the best order in which to put the sentences so as to form a well-organized paragraph.

The questions in this section measure the ability to solve a problem when all the facts relevant to its solution are not given.

More specifically, certain positions of responsibility and authority require the employee to discover connection between events sometimes, apparently, unrelated. In order to do this, the employee will find it necessary to correctly infer that unspecified events have probably occurred or are likely to occur. This ability becomes especially important when action must be taken on incomplete information.

Accordingly, these questions require competitors to choose among several suggested alternatives, each of which presents a different sequential arrangement of the events. Competitors must choose the MOST logical of the suggested sequences.

In order to do so, they may be required to draw on general knowledge to infer missing concepts or events that are essential to sequencing the given events. Competitors should be careful to infer only what is essential to the sequence. The plausibility of the wrong alternatives will always require the inclusion of unlikely events or of additional chains of events which are NOT essential to sequencing the given events.

It's very important to remember that you are looking for the best of the four possible choices, and that the best choice of all may not even be one of the answers you're given to choose from.

There is no one right way to solve these problems. Many people have found it helpful to first write out the order of the sentences, as they would have arranged them, on their scrap paper before looking at the possible answers. If their optimum answer is there, this can save them some time. If it isn't, this method can still give insight into solving the problem. Others find it most helpful to just go through each of the possible choices, contrasting each as they go along. You should use whatever method feels comfortable and works for you.

While most of these types of questions are not that difficult, we've added a higher percentage of the difficult type, just to give you more practice. Usually there are only one or two questions on this section that contain such subtle distinctions that you're unable to answer confidently. And you then may find yourself stuck deciding between two possible choices, neither of which you're sure about.

EXAMINATION SECTION
TEST 1

DIRECTIONS: Each question consists of several sentences which can be arranged in a logical sequence. For each question, select the choice which places the numbered sentences in the MOST logical sequence. *PRINT THE LETTER OF THE CORRECT ANSWER IN THE SPACE AT THE RIGHT.*

1. I. A body was found in the woods.
   II. A man proclaimed innocence.
   III. The owner of a gun was located.
   IV. A gun was traced.
   V. The owner of a gun was questioned.
   The CORRECT answer is:
   A. IV, III, V, II, I
   B. II, I, IV, III, V
   C. I, IV, III, V, II
   D. I, III, V, II, IV
   E. I, II, IV, III, V

   1.____

2. I. A man is in a hunting accident.
   II. A man fell down a flight of steps.
   III. A man lost his vision in one eye,
   IV. A man broke his leg.
   V. A man had to walk with a cane.
   The CORRECT answer is:
   A. II, IV, V, I, III
   B. IV, V, I, III, II
   C. III, I, IV, V, II
   D. I, III, V, II, IV
   E. I, III, II, IV, V

   2.____

3. I. A man is offered a new job.
   II. A woman is offered a new job.
   III. A man works as a waiter.
   IV. A woman works as a waitress.
   V. A woman gives notice.
   The CORRECT answer is:
   A. IV, II, V, III, I
   B. IV, II, V, I, III
   C. II, IV, V, III, I
   D. III, I, IV, II, V
   E. IV, III, II, V, I

   3.____

4. I. A train let the station late.
   II. A man was late for work.
   III. A man lost his job.
   IV. Many people complained because the train was late.
   V. There was a traffic jam.
   The CORRECT answer is:
   A. V, II, I, IV, III
   B. V, I, IV, II, III
   C. V, I, II, IV, III
   D. I, V, IV, II, III
   E. II, I, IV, V, III

   4.____

5. I. The burden of proof as to each issue is determined before trial and remains upon the same party throughout the trial.
    II. The jury is at liberty to believe one witness' testimony as against a number of contradictory witnesses.
    III. In a civil case, the party bearing the burden of proof is required to prove his contention by a fair preponderance of the evidence.
    IV. However, it must be noted that a fair preponderance of evidence does not necessarily mean a greater number of witnesses.
    V. The burden of proof is the burden which rests upon one of the parties to an action to persuade the trier of the facts, generally the jury, that a proposition he asserts is true.
    VI. If the evidence is equally balanced, or if it leaves the jury in such doubt as to be unable to decide the controversy either way, judgment must be given against the party upon whom the burden of proof rests.
    The CORRECT answer is:
    A. III. II, V, IV, I, VI   B. I, II, VI, V, III, IV   C. III, IV, V, I, II, VI
    D. V, I, III, VI, IV, II   E. I, V, III, VI, IV, II

6. I. If a parent is without assets and is unemployed, he cannot be convicted of the crime of non-support of a child.
    II. The term *sufficient ability* has been held to mean sufficient financial ability.
    III. It does not matter if his unemployment is by choice or unavoidable circumstances.
    IV. If he fails to take any steps at all, he may be liable to prosecution for endangering the welfare of a child.
    V. Under the penal law, a parent is responsible for the support of his minor child only if the parent is of *sufficient ability*.
    VI. An indigent parent may meet his obligation by borrowing money or by seeking aid under the provisions of the Social Welfare Law.
    The CORRECT answer is:
    A. VI, I, V, III, II, IV   B. I, III, V, II, IV, VI   C. V, II, I, III, VI, IV
    D. I, VI, IV, V, II, III   E. II, V, I, III, VI, IV

7. I. Consider, for example, the case of a rabble rouser who urges a group of twenty people to go out and break the windows of a nearby factory.
    II. Therefore, the law fills the indicated gap with the crime of *inciting to riot*.
    III. A person is considered guilty of inciting to riot when he urges ten or more persons to engage in tumultuous and violent conduct of a kind likely to create public alarm.
    IV. However, if he has not obtained the cooperation of at least four people, he cannot be charged with unlawful assembly.
    V. The charge of inciting to riot was added to the law to cover types of conduct which cannot be classified as either the crime of *riot* or the crime of *unlawful assembly*.
    VI. If he acquires the acquiescence of at least four of them, he is guilty of unlawful assembly even if the project does not materialize.
    The CORRECT answer is:
    A. III, V, I, VI, IV, II   B. V, I, IV, VI, II, III   C. III, IV, I, V, II, VI
    D. V, I, IV, VI, III, II   E. V, III, I, VI, IV, II

8. I. If, however, the rebuttal evidence presents an issue of credibility, it is for the jury to determine whether the presumption has, in fact, been destroyed.
    II. Once sufficient evidence to the contrary is introduced, the presumption disappears from the trial.
    III. The effect of a presumption is to place the burden upon the adversary to come forward with evidence to rebut the presumption.
    IV. When a presumption is overcome and ceases to exist in the case, the fact or facts which gave rise to the presumption still remain.
    V. Whether a presumption has been overcome is ordinarily a question for the court.
    VI. Such information may furnish a basis for a logical inference.
    The CORRECT answer is:
    A. IV, VI, II, V, I, III   B. III, II, V, I, IV, VI   C. V, III, VI, IV, II, I
    D. V, IV, I, II, VI, III   E. II, III, V, I, IV, VI

9. I. An executive may answer a letter by writing his reply on the face of the letter itself instead of having a return letter typed.
    II. This procedure is efficient because it saves the executive's time, the typist's time, and saves office file space.
    III. Copying machines are used in small offices as well as large offices to save time and money in making brief replies to business letters.
    IV. A copy is made on a copying machine to go into the company files, while the original is mailed back to the sender.
    The CORRECT answer is:
    A. I, II, IV, III   B. I, IV, II, III   C. III, I, IV, II   D. III, IV, II, I

10. I. Most organizations favor one of the types but always include the others to a lesser degree.
    II. However, we can detect a definite trend toward greater use of symbolic control.
    III. We suggest that our local police agencies are today primarily utilizing material control.
    IV. Control can be classified into three types: physical, material, and symbolic.
    The CORRECT answer is:
    A. IV, II, III, I   B. II, I, IV, III   C. III, IV, II, I   D. IV, I, III, II

11. I. Project residents had first claim to this use, followed by surrounding neighborhood children.
    II. By contrast, recreation space within the project's interior was found to be used more often by both groups.
    III. Studies of the use of project grounds in many cities showed grounds left open for public use were neglected and unused, both by residents and by members of the surrounding community.
    IV. Project residents had clearly laid claim to the play spaces, setting up and enforcing unwritten rules for use.
    V. Each group, by experience, found their activities easily disrupted by other groups, and their claim to the use of space for recreation difficult to enforce.

The CORRECT answer is:
A. IV, V, I, II, III
B. V, II, IV, III, I
C. I, IV, III, II, V
D. III, V, II, IV, I

12. I. They do not consider the problems correctable within the existing subsidy formula and social policy of accepting all eligible applicants regardless of social behavior.
    II. A recent survey, however, indicated that tenants believe these problems correctable by local housing authorities and management within the existing financial formula.
    III. Many of the problems and complaints concerning public housing management and design have created resentment between the tenant and the landlord.
    IV. This same survey indicated that administrators and managers do not agree with the tenants.
    The CORRECT answer is:
    A. II, I, III, IV
    B. I, III, IV, II
    C. III, II, IV, I
    D. IV, II, I, III

13. I. In single-family residences, there is usually enough distance between tenants to prevent occupants from annoying one another.
    II. For example, a certain small percentage of tenant families has one or more members addicted to alcohol.
    III. While managers believe in the right of individuals to live as they choose, the manager becomes concerned when the pattern of living jeopardizes others' rights.
    IV. Still others turn night into day, staging lusty entertainments which carry on into the hours when most tenants are trying to sleep.
    V. In apartment buildings, however, tenants live so closely together that any misbehavior can result in unpleasant living conditions.
    VI. Other families engage in violent argument.
    The CORRECT answer is:
    A. III, II, V, IV, VI, I
    B. I, V, II, VI, IV, III
    C. II, V, IV, I, III, VI
    D. IV, II, V, VI, III, I

14. I. Congress made the commitment explicit in the Housing Act of 194, establishing as a national goal the realization of a *decent home and suitable environment for every American family*.
    II. The result has been that the goal of decent home and suitable environment is still as far distant as ever for the disadvantaged urban family.
    III. In spite of this action by Congress, federal housing programs have continued to be fragmented and grossly underfunded.
    IV. The passage of the National Housing Act signaled a few federal commitment to provide housing for the nation's citizens.
    The CORRECT answer is:
    A. I, IV, III, II
    B. IV, I, III, II
    C. IV, I, II, III
    D. II, IV, I, III

15. I. The greater expense does not necessarily involve *exploitation*, but it is often perceived as exploitative and unfair by those who are aware of the price differences involved, but unaware of operating costs.
   II. Ghetto residents believe they are *exploited* by local merchants, and evidence substantiates some of these beliefs.
   III. However, stores in low-income areas were more likely to be small independents, which could not achieve the economies available to supermarket chains and were, therefore, more likely to charge higher prices, and the customers were more likely to buy smaller-sized packages which are more expensive per unit of measure.
   IV. A study conducted in one city showed that distinctly higher prices were charged for goods sold in ghetto stores in other areas.
   The CORRECT answer is:
   A. IV, II, I, III   B. IV, I, III, II   C. II, IV, III, I   D. II, III, IV, I

15.____

KEY (CORRECT ANSWERS)

1.	C	6.	C	11.	D
2.	E	7.	A	12.	C
3.	B	8.	B	13.	B
4.	B	9.	C	14.	B
5.	D	10.	D	15.	C

PREPARING WRITTEN MATERIALS
EXAMINATION SECTION
TEST 1

DIRECTIONS: Each question or incomplete statement is followed by several suggested answers or completions. Select the one that BEST answers the question or completes the statement. *PRINT THE LETTER OF THE CORRECT ANSWER IN THE SPACE AT THE RIGHT.*

Questions 1-25.

DIRECTIONS: Questions 1 through 25 consist of sentences which may or may not be examples of good English usage. Consider grammar, punctuation, spelling, capitalization, awkwardness, etc. Examine each sentence and then choose the correct statement about it from the four choices below it. If the English usage in the sentence given is better than it would be with any of the changes suggested in options B, C, and D, choose option A. Do not choose an option that will change the meaning of the sentence.

1. According to Judge Frank, the grocer's sons found guilty of assault and sentenced last Thursday.
    A. This is an example of acceptable writing.
    B. A comma should be placed after the word *sentenced*.
    C. The word *were* should be placed after *sons*.
    D. The apostrophe in grocer's should be placed after the *s*.

1.____

2. The department heads assistant said that the stenographers should type duplicate copies of all contracts, leases, and bills.
    A. This is an example of acceptable writing,
    B. A comma should be placed before the word "*contracts.*
    C. An apostrophe should be placed before the *s* in *heads*.
    D. Quotation marks should be placed before the *stenographers* and after *bills*.

2.____

3. The lawyers questioned the men to determine who was the true property owner?
    A. This is an example of acceptable writing.
    B. The phrase *questioned the men* should be changed to *asked the men questions*.
    C. The word *was* should be changed to *were*.
    D. The question mark should be changed to a period.

3.____

4. The terms stated in the present contract are more specific than those stated in the previous contract.
   A. This is an example of acceptable writing,
   B. The word *are* should be changed to *is*.
   C. The word *than* should be changed to *then*.
   D. The word *specific* should be changed to *specified*.

   4.____

5. Of the few lawyers considered, the one who argued more skillful was chosen for the job.
   A. This is an example of acceptable writing.
   B. The word *more* should be replaced by the word *most*.
   C. The word *skillful* should be replaced by the word *skillfully*.
   D. The word *chosen* should be replaced by the word *selected*.

   5.____

6. Each of the states has a court of appeals; some states have circuit courts.
   A. This is an example of acceptable writing
   B. The semi-colon should be changed to a comma.
   C. The word *has* should be changed to *have*.
   D. The word *some* should be capitalized.

   6.____

7. The court trial has greatly effected the child's mental condition.
   A. This is an example of acceptable writing.
   B. The word *effected* should be changed to *affected*.
   C. The word *greatly* should be placed after *effected*.
   D. The apostrophe in *child's* should be placed after the *s*.

   7.____

8. Last week, the petition signed by all the officers was sent to the Better Business Bureau.
   A. This is an example of acceptable writing.
   B. The phrase *last week* should be placed after *officers*.
   C. A comma should be placed after *petition*.
   D. The word *was* should be changed to *were*.

   8.____

9. Mr. Farrell claims that he requested form A-12, and three booklets describing court procedures.
   A. This is an example of acceptable writing.
   B. The word *that* should be eliminated.
   C. A colon should be placed after *requested*.
   D. The comma after *A-12* should be eliminated.

   9.____

10. We attended a staff conference on Wednesday the new safety and fire rules were discussed.
    A. This is an example of acceptable writing.
    B. The words *safety*, *fire*, and *rules* should begin with capital letters.
    C. There should be a comma after the word *Wednesday*.
    D. There should be a period after the word *Wednesday*, and the word *the* should begin with a capital letter.

    10.____

11. Neither the dictionary or the telephone directory could be found in the office library.   11.____
    A. This is an example of acceptable writing.
    B. The word *or* should be changed to *nor*.
    C. The word *library* should be spelled *libery*.
    D. The word *neither* should be changed to *either*.

12. The report would have been typed correctly if the typist could read the draft.   12.____
    A. This is an example of acceptable writing.
    B. The word *would* should be removed.
    C. The word *have* should be inserted after the word *could*.
    D. The word *correctly* should be changed to *correct*.

13. The supervisor brought the reports and forms to an employees desk.   13.____
    A. This is an example of acceptable writing.
    B. The word *brought* should be changed to *took*.
    C. There should be a comma after the word *reports* and a comma after the word *forms*.
    D. The word *employees* should be spelled *employee's*.

14. It's important for all the office personnel to submit their vacation schedules on time.   14.____
    A. This is an example of acceptable writing.
    B. The word *It's* should be spelled *Its*.
    C. The word *their* should be spelled *they're*.
    D. The word *personnel* should be spelled *personal*.

15. The supervisor wants that all staff members report to the office at 9:00 A.M.   15.____
    A. This is an example of acceptable writing.
    B. The word *that* should be removed and the word *to* should be inserted after the word *members*.
    C. There should be a comma after the word *wants* and a comma after the word *office*.
    D. The word *wants* should be changed to *want* and the word *shall* should be inserted after the word *members*.

16. Every morning the clerk opens the office mail and distributes it.   16.____
    A. This is an example of acceptable writing.
    B. The word *opens* should be changed to *letters*.
    C. The word *mail* should be changed to *letters*.
    D. The word *it* should be changed to *them*.

17. The secretary typed more fast on a desktop computer than on a tablet.   17.____
    A. This is an example of acceptable writing.
    B. The words *more fast* should be changed to *faster*.
    C. There should be a comma after the words *desktop computer*.
    D. The word *than* should be changed to *then*.

18. The typist used an extention cord in order to connect her typewriter to the outlet nearest to her desks.
    A. This is an example of acceptable writing.
    B. A period should be placed after the word *cord*, and the word *in* should have a capital *I*.
    C. A comma should be placed after the word *typewriter*.
    D. The word *extention* should be spelled *extension*.

19. He would have went to the conference if he had received an invitation.
    A. This is an example of acceptable writing.
    B. The word *went* should be replaced by the word *gone*.
    C. The word *had* should be replaced by *would have*.
    D. The word *conference* should be spelled *conferance*.

20. In order to make the report neater, he spent many hours rewriting it.
    A. This is an example of acceptable writing.
    B. The word *more* should be inserted before the word *neater*.
    C. There should be a colon after the word *neater*.
    D. The word *spent* should be changed to *have spent*.

21. His supervisor told him that he should of read the memorandum more carefully.
    A. This is an example of acceptable writing.
    B. The word *memorandum* should be spelled *memorandom*.
    C. The word *of* should be replaced by the word *have*.
    D. The word *carefully* should be replaced by the word *careful*.

22. It was decided that two separate reports should be written.
    A. This is an example of acceptable writing.
    B. A comma should be inserted after the word *decided*.
    C. The word *be* should be replaced by the word *been*.
    D. A colon should be inserted after the word *that*.

23. She don't seem to understand that the work must be done as soon as possible.
    A. This is an example of acceptable writing.
    B. The word *doesn't* should replace the word *don't*.
    C. The word *why* should replace the word *that*.
    D. The word *as* before the word *soon* should be eliminated.

24. He excepted praise from his supervisor for a job well done.
    A. This is an example of acceptable writing.
    B. The word *excepted* should be spelled *accepted*.
    C. The order of the words *well done* should be changed to *done well*.
    D. There should be a comma after the word *supervisor*.

25. What appears to be intentional errors in grammar occur several times in the passage.   25._____
    A. This is an example of acceptable writing.
    B. The word *occur* should be spelled *occur*.
    C. The word *appears* should be changed to *appear*.
    D. The phrase *several times* should be changed to *from time to time*.

KEY (CORRECT ANSWERS)

1.	C		11.	B
2.	C		12.	C
3.	D		13.	D
4.	A		14.	A
5.	C		15.	B
6.	A		16.	A
7.	B		17.	B
8.	A		18.	D
9.	D		19.	B
10.	D		20.	A

21. C
22. A
23. B
24. B
25. C

TEST 2

DIRECTIONS: Each question consists of a sentence which may or may not be an example of good formal English usage. Examine each sentence, considering grammar, punctuation, spelling, capitalization, and awkwardness. Then choose the CORRECT statement about it from the four options below it. If the English usage in the sentence given is better than any of the changes suggested in options B, C, or D, pick option A. Do not pick an option that will change the meaning of the sentence. *PRINT THE LETTER OF THE CORRECT ANSWER IN THE SPACE AT THE RIGHT.*

1. I don't know who could possibly of broken it. 1.____
   A. This is an example of acceptable writing.
   B. The word *who* should be replaced by the word *whom*.
   C. The word *of* should be replaced by the word *have*.
   D. The word *broken* should be replaced by the word *broke*.

2. Telephoning is easier than to write. 2.____
   A. This is an example of acceptable writing.
   B. The word *telephoning* should be spelled *telephoneing*.
   C. The word *than* should be replaced by the word *then*.
   D. The words *to write* should be replaced by the word *writing*.

3. The two operators who have been assigned to these consoles are on vacation. 3.____
   A. This is an example of acceptable writing.
   B. A comma should be placed after the word *operators*.
   C. The word *who* should be replaced by the word *whom*.
   D. The word *are* should be replaced by the word *is*.

4. You were suppose to teach me how to operate a plugboard. 4.____
   A. This is an example of acceptable writing,
   B. The word *were* should be replaced by the word *was*.
   C. The word *suppose* should be replaced by the word *supposed*.
   D. The word *teach* should be replaced by the word *team*.

5. If you had taken my advice; you would have spoken with him. 5.____
   A. This is an example of acceptable writing.
   B. The word *advice* should be spelled *advise*.
   C. The words *had taken* should be replaced by the word *take*.
   D. The semicolon should be changed to a comma.

6. The clerk could have completed the assignment on time if he knows where these materials were located. 6.____
   A. This is an example of acceptable writing.
   B. The word *knows* should be replaced by *had known*.
   C. The word "were" should be replaced by *had been*.
   D. The words *where these materials were located* should be replaced by *the location of these materials*.

2 (#2)

7. All employees should be given safety training. Not just those who have accidents.
   A. This is an example of acceptable writing,
   B. The period after the word *training* should be changed to a colon.
   C. The period after the word *training* should be changed to a semicolon, and the first letter of the word *Not* should be changed to a small *n*.
   D. The period after the word *training* should be changed to a comma, and the first letter of the word *Not* should be changed to a small *n*,

7.____

8. This proposal is designed to promote employee awareness of the suggestion program, to encourage employee participation in the program, and to increase the number of suggestions submitted.
   A. This is an example of acceptable writing.
   B. The word *proposal* should be spelled *proposal*.
   C. The words *to increase the number of suggestions submitted* should be changed to *an increase in the number of suggestions is expected*.
   D. The word *promote* should be changed to *enhance*, and the word *increase* should be changed to *add to*.

8.____

9. The introduction of inovative managerial techniques should be preceded by careful analysis of the specific circumstances and conditions in each department.
   A. This is an example of acceptable writing.
   B. The word *techniques* should be spelled *techneques*.
   C. The word *inovative* should be spelled *innovative*.
   D. A comma should be placed after the word *circumstances* and after the word *conditions*.

9.____

10. This occurrence indicates that such criticism embarrasses him.
    A. This is an example of acceptable writing.
    B. The word *occurrence* should be spelled *occurence*.
    C. The word *criticism* should be spelled *creticism*.
    D. The word *embarrasses* should be spelled *embarasses*.

10.____

11. He can recommend a mechanic whose work is reliable.
    A. This is an example of acceptable writing.
    B. the word *reliable* should be spelled *relyable*.
    C. The word *whose* should be spelled *who's*.
    D. The word *mechanic* should be spelled *mecanic*.

11.____

12. She typed quickly; like someone who had not a moment to lose.
    A. This is an example of acceptable writing.
    B. The word *not* should be removed.
    C. The semicolon should be changed to a comma.
    D. The word *quickly* should be placed before instead of after the word *typed*.

12.____

13. She insisted that she had to much work to do. 13._____
    A. This is an example of acceptable writing.
    B. The word *insisted* should be spelled *insisted*.
    C. The word *to* used in front of *much* should be spelled *too*.
    D. The word *do* should be changed to *be done*.

14. The report, along with the accompanying documents, were submitted for 14._____
    review.
    A. This is an example of acceptable writing.
    B. The words *were submitted* should be changed to *was submitted*.
    C. The word *accompanying* should be spelled *accompaning*.
    D. The comma after the word *report* should be taken out.

15. If others must use your files, be certain that they understand how the system 15._____
    works, but insist that you do all the filing and refiling.
    A. This is an example of acceptable writing.
    B. There should be a period after the word *works*, and the word *but* should
       start a new sentence.
    C. The words *filing* and *refiling* should be spelled *fileing* and *refileing*.
    D. There should be a comma after the word *but*.

16. The appeal was not considered because of its late arrival. 16._____
    A. This is an example of acceptable writing.
    B. The word *its* should be changed to *it's*.
    C. The word *its* should be changed to *the*.
    D. The words *late arrival* should be changed to *arrival late*.

17. The letter must be read carefully to determine under which subject it should 17._____
    be filed.
    A. This is an example of acceptable writing.
    B. The word *under* should be changed to *at*.
    C. The word *determine* should be spelled *determin*.
    D. The word *carefully* should be spelled *carefuly*.

18. He showed potential as an office manager, but he lacked skill in delegating 18._____
    work.
    A. This is an example of acceptable writing.
    B. The word *delegating* should be spelled *delagating*.
    C. The word *potential* should be spelled *potencial*.
    D. The words *he lacked* should be changed to *was lacking*.

19. His supervisor told him that it would be all right to receive personal mail at 19._____
    the office.
    A. This is an example of acceptable writing.
    B. The words *all right* should be changed to *alright*.
    C. The word *personal* should be spelled *personel*.
    D. The word *mail* should be changed to *letters*.

20. The report, along with the accompanying documents, were submitted for review. 20.____
    A. This is an example of acceptable writing.
    B. The words *were submitted* should be changed to *was submitted*.
    C. The word *accompanying* should be spelled *accompaning*.
    D. The comma after the word *report* should be taken out.

KEY (CORRECT ANSWERS)

1.	C	11.	A
2.	D	12.	C
3.	A	13.	C
4.	C	14.	B
5.	D	15.	A
6.	B	16.	A
7.	D	17.	D
8.	A	18.	A
9.	C	19.	A
10.	A	20.	B

MENTAL DISORDERS AND TREATMENT PRACTICES

This section reviews eight areas that are usually tested on examinations:

- The Characteristics of Various Psychiatric Disorders
- The Needs of Special Groups (Children, Geriatrics)
- The Influences of Environment, Society, and Family on Psychiatric Disorders
- Psychotropic Drugs (Reactions and Uses)
- The Assessment and Evaluation of Patients
- The Functions and Purposes of the Treatment Team
- The Development and Implementation of the Treatment Plan
- Methods for Handling People with Various Emotional or Psychiatric Disorders

THE CHARACTERISTICS OF VARIOUS PSYCHIATRIC DISORDERS

It is often difficult to assign labels to human behavior with any large degree of accuracy. Behavior sometimes changes rapidly, and the interpretation of what behavior a label actually represents can vary greatly from one person to the next. One can often learn a great deal more about a person by observing their behavior than by reading a diagnostic label about that person. Regardless, diagnostic labels can be helpful to members of a treatment team as a shorthand method of describing a group of behaviors one might expect from certain individuals. They are also required for many insurance forms. A diagnosis may be useful as long as one views the diagnosis as an ongoing process, and can continue to look at the patient with *new eyes*.

The Difference Between Neurosis and Psychosis

People suffering from a neurosis are usually able to manage with the concerns of daily life, although there is often some distortion in their concept of reality. Those suffering from a neurosis may feel inferior, unloved, or have a long-term feeling of fear or dread. They may have obsessions, compulsions or phobias, but they are rarely dangerous to themselves or others. They usually have some insight into their problems, and except in severe cases, don't require hospitalization. Many go through life without obtaining any help for their problems. Those who experience a psychosis, however, are out of touch with reality and live in an imaginary world. They may hear voices, feel that they are being persecuted, or experience very deep depressions. There is a very definite split between the reality of those suffering from psychoses and the reality of the world. Unlike those suffering from neuroses, those suffering from psychoses often lose track of time, person, and place, and they have little insight into the nature of their behavior. They usually require hospitalization and their behavior is sometimes injurious to other people or themselves, although they may insist that there is nothing wrong with them.

Categories of Neurosis

It is important to keep in mind that rarely will all of a patient's symptoms fall into any one category, and that symptoms may change over time from one category to another. *Anxiety Neuroses* constitute approximately 35% of all neurotic disorders. Those suffering from anxiety neuroses have a tendency to view the world as hostile and cruel, and may frequently restrict daily activities in order to feel safer in their environment. They often feel tense, worried, and anxious, but are unable to articulate exactly why they feel this way. Many anxious individuals are very uncertain of themselves in even minor stress producing situations, and they may have real difficulties in concentrating because of their high anxiety levels.

Other symptoms may include strong anxiety reactions with difficulty catching one's breath, perspiration, increased heart beat, dizziness, and feeling that they are dying. They may come to the Emergency Room of a hospital complaining of a heart attack or heart troubles. It is important to keep in mind that many elements of the anxiety reaction are seen in patients with other neurotic disorders.

Conversion Reactions or *Hysteria* involve the loss of ability to perform some physical function that the person could previously perform, which is psychogenic in origin. This reaction is an attempt by the individual to defend herself or himself from some anxiety producing situation by developing physical symptoms that have no organic or physical cause. These reactions are not common, and constitute less than five percent of neurotic disorders. The lost function is often symbolically related to a situation which has produced stress or anxiety, and is often an attempt to escape from that situation. The person may lose the ability to hear or speak, have unusual bodily sensations, or lose control of some motor function. Since there is no physical cause of dysfunction, some people assume that the pain or paralysis is not real, or that this type of person is faking. *Dissociative Reactions* also serve to protect the individual from particularly stressful situations. Amnesia, fugue, and multiple personalities are the major categories of dissociative reactions. Despite the prevalence of *amnesia* on soap operas, dissociative reactions account for less than five percent of all neurotic disorders. Amnesiacs usually forget specific information for a specified but variable period of time. The patient does not, however, forget his or her basic lifestyle or habits. In *fugue,* the person combines the amnesia with flight, and leaves the area where the stressful situation is. Usually the person is unaware of where he or she has been, or where he or she is going. There are very few cases of *multiple personalities.* In this disorder, the person shows different ways of responding to the environment. Each individual personality within the person is a complete personality system, and may dominate the person's reactions to his or her environment, depending upon the situation.

Obsessive-Compulsive Reactions involve either the inability to stop thinking about something the person does not want to think about, or the obligatory performance of a repetitive act. People experiencing these reactions often recognize they are irrational, but are unable to stop doing them. They often attempt to rearrange their environment, which they may perceive as threatening, in an attempt to impose control and structure, so they can control their environment and feel safer. Those suffering from compulsive reactions feel a strong need to perform or repeat certain behaviors, often in order to prevent something terrible from happening to them. (This might involve pre-determined ways to enter a room, brush their teeth, get into bed, begin conversations, etc.) Of course, many people may exhibit aspects of this behavior. Observing some professional baseball players before they pitch or take a pitch can certainly demonstrate this point. There is little cause for concern if the patterns are relatively temporary and help the person in some way obtain their goal. When the behaviors begin to unduly restrict a person's activities, then the situation becomes more serious. People exhibiting this behavior are often unable to make decisions effectively, are often perfectionists, have a strong need for structure, and are fairly rigid. Those who are obsessed with unwanted thoughts may have quite a variety of areas that they think about. The most common areas, however, concern religion, ethical concerns (something being absolutely right or wrong), bodily functions, and suicide.

Phobic Reactions involve a strong, persistent irrational fear of an object, condition, or place. It is believed that phobias usually involve a displacement of anxiety from the original cause to the phobic object. The phobia serves to assist the individual in avoiding the anxiety-causing situation. Some of the most common phobias include fear of crowds, being alone, darkness, thunderstorms, and high places. It is often very difficult to discover the symbolic significance of a particular phobia.

Neurotic Depressive Reactions involve an intensification of normal grief reactions. Research has indicated that those suffering from this reaction are unable to *bounce back* from upsetting or discouraging events. People who suffer from this reaction tend to have a poor self-concept, exaggerated dependency needs, a tendency to feel guilty about almost anything, and to turn those guilt feelings against themselves in a highly punitive way. The possibility of suicide should be kept in mind when working with these patients.

Categories of Psychosis

Psychoses are generally divided into two categories, *functional psychoses* and *organic psychoses*. Functional psychoses are caused by psychological stress, while organic psychoses are caused by a disorder of the brain for which physical pathology can be demonstrated. A third category, *toxic psychoses,* is sometimes used to refer to psychotic reactions caused by toxic substances such as drugs or poisons.

Schizophrenia accounts for approximately 25 percent of all first admissions to mental institutions, and is the largest single diagnostic group of psychotic patients. The *paranoid schizophrenic* shows a great deal of suspiciousness and hostility, and may be very aggressive. The *simple type schizophrenic* is shy and withdrawn, and shows interest in his or her environment. The *hebephrenic schizophrenic* often has bizarre mannerisms and may appear quite manic. He or she may laugh and giggle inappropriately, and become preoccupied with unimportant matters. The *catatonic schizophrenic* may remain motionless for days or hours, and may refuse to eat. The two phases of catatonia are the *stuporous phase* where the person is motionless and *catatonic excitement* where the person is over-active and appears manic. While the catatonic schizophrenic may alternate between these two phases, most show a preference for just one. Someone suffering from *schizoaffective schizophrenia* will have significant thought disorders and mood variations. They may initially appear to be depressed or manic, but a basic personality disorganization also exists. These are the major categories of schizophrenia you should need for the exam. Since the exam announcement states basic knowledge is required, it is very possible some of the above categories may be too specific. We have included them just in case, however.

The general symptoms of schizophrenia include an inability to deal with reality, the presence of hallucinations or delusions, inappropriate emotions, autism and various other unusual behaviors. There is often a very noticeable inability to organize thoughts. Schizophrenic reactions that occur suddenly are referred to as *acute* schizophrenic reactions, while those that develop slowly over a rather lengthy period are called *chronic* schizophrenic reactions.

Paranoid Reactions in people account for less than one percent of psychiatric admissions. Those with this behavior usually mistrust the motives of everyone, are very resentful, and often hostile. They may show signs of grandiosity or persecution. The person often believes that whatever happens is related to him or her. The major difference between paranoid patients and paranoid schizophrenics is that the paranoid patient usually has better control of his or her thought processes, and is able to make more appropriate responses to situations. They are usually more reality-oriented, and able to state their feelings more effectively.

Affective Reactions are those that represent a change in the normal affect, or mood, of a person. There are two major categories of affective disorders: *manic-depressive reactions* and *involutional psychotic reactions.* In the manic-depressive reaction, the manic and depressive states alternate. In the manic phase, the person may be extremely talkative, agitated or elated, and demonstrate a great deal of physical and verbal activity. They may also exhibit some grandiosity. In the depressive phase, the person is joyless, quiet, and inhibited. The manic reactions are often divided into three degress of severity, each category representing a more severe degree of manic reaction. *Hypomania* is the least severe, *acute mania* is the next, and *delirious mania* is the most severe state. The term *involutional psychosis is* usually related to a patient's age. For women, the involutional age is considered to be somewhere between 40 and 55, and the involutional period for men is somewhere between 50 and 65. It seems that stresses are greater for men and women during these periods, and that these stresses may trigger psychotic reactions which are generally transient. These people generally have a long history of feeling guilty and very anxious, have little diversity of activity, and few sources of satisfaction in their lives.

Selected Personality Disorders

This category includes behavior which is maladaptive, but neither psychotic nor neurotic. This group includes *antisocial reactions,* the *abuse of alchol and other drugs,* and *sexual deviations.* The *antisocial* or *sociopathic* personality type fails to develop a concern for others and uses relationships to get what he or she wants. There is little or no concern about what effect their behavior might have on others, and they seldom feel remorse or guilt. They are often likable, friendly, intelligent people. Their relationships with others tend to be superficial, however, because they lack the capacity for deep emotional responses. The sociopath is often impulsive and seeks immediate gratification of his or her wants. He or she often is unreliable, untruthful, undependable and insincere. A large number of people have sociopathic traits which, as with most other characteristics, vary in severity and number. Sociopaths are found in all professions, although many are able to control their acting out behaviors or channel them in more socially acceptable ways. They avoid acting out not because of internal values, but because they do not wish to get caught. Sociopaths usually have a low frustration tolerance, are easily bored, and continually seek excitement. The sociopath most frequently comes to treatment because he or she has been *caught* doing something or been required to seek help by an employer or family member.

Sexual Deviations occur in those who fail to develop what their society considers appropriate sexual behavior. The major sexual deviations include child molestation, rape, sadism, masochism, voyeurism, fetishism, transvestism, exhibitionism, pedophilia, and incest. As you can see, some of these behaviors are much more harmful to other people than others are.

PSYCHOTROPIC DRUGS (REACTIONS AND USES)

The two major classifications of the psychotropic drugs are the tranquilizers, which are further divided into major (or anti-psychotic) and minor (or antianxiety) groups, and the antidepressants. Other drugs used include anticonvulsants, sedatives, hypnotics, and antiparkinsons.

Tranquilizers are meant to calm disturbed patients, and free them from agitation or disturbance. Drugs designed as *antipsychotic,* or *major tranquilizers,* also help to reduce the frequency of hallucinations, delusions, thought disorders, and the type of withdrawal seen in catatonic schizophrenia. It may take several days of drug therapy before the symptoms begin to subside, but during this time the patient becomes less fearful, hostile and upset by his disturbed sensory perceptions. The *phenothiazine derivatives* are the largest group of antipsychotic drugs. All the drugs in this group have essentially the same type of action on the body, but vary according to strength and the type and severity of their side effects. These drugs include:

Thorazine	Trilafon	Taractan
Mellaril	Compazine	Navane
Stelazine	Dartal	Sordinal
Prolixin	Proketazine	Haldol
Sparine	Tindal	Loxitane
Vesprin	Repoise	Moban

Serious side effects are very important to watch for. For these drugs, the phenothiazine derivatives, there are three major types of extrapyramidal symptoms (EPS): (1) akinesia - inability to sit still, complaints of fatigue and weakness, and continuous movement of the hands, mouth, and body; (2) pseudoparkinsonism -restlessness, mask-like facial expressions, drooling, and tremors; (3) tardive dyskenesia - lack of control over voluntary movements. Symptoms may include involuntary grimacing, sucking and chewing movements, pursing of the tongue and mouth, jerking of the hands, feet and neck, and drooping head. Immediate action must be taken to combat these side effects. The administration of antiparkinson drugs usually produces a dramatic reduction in symptoms. Unless spotted and treated early, however, these can become permanent.

Other side effects may include muscle spasms, shuffling gait, skin rash, eye problems, trembling hands and fingers, fainting, wormlike tongue movements, sore throat and fever, yellowing of skin or eyes, dry mouth, constipation, excessive weight gain, edema, a drop in blood pressure when moving from a lying to standing position, decreased sexual interest, sensitivity to light and prone to sunburn and visual problems, blurred vision, drowsiness, and increased perspiration. Just about any physical symptom or behavior could be caused by a reaction to a drug.

Special Considerations: Patients receiving a high dose of a phenothiazine drug should have their blood pressure checked regularly. Long exposures of skin to sunlight should be avoided (a wide-brimmed hat and long-sleeved clothing can also help). If a patient receiving phenothiazines is lethargic and wants to sleep a great deal, the dose of the drug may be too high and need adjustment. Patients on phenothiazines should not drive or use dangerous equipment. These drugs greatly increase the effects of alcohol. In the first three to five days, a person may feel drowsy and dizzy upon standing. Antipsychotic drugs tend to mask the symptoms of diseases and dictate that patients receiving them undergo thorough physical examinations every six months.

The *Minor Tranquilizers*, or *antianxiety drugs*, reduce anxiety and muscle tension associated with it. They are useful primarily with psychoneurotic and psychosomatic disorders. When given in small doses, they are relatively safe and have few side effects. Unlike the antipsychotic drugs, some of the antianxiety drugs tend to be habit-forming. If the drug is discontinued, the person may experience severe withdrawal symptoms, such as convulsions or delirium. These drugs include:

Librium	Milpath	Frienquel
Azene	Deprol	Phobex
Tranxene	Milprem	Softran
Valium	Miltown	Atarax
Ativan	Robaxin	Vistaril
Serax	Solacen	Trancopal

Side effects may include rashes, chills, fever, nausea, headaches, poor muscle coordination, some inability to concentrate, and dizziness. Excessive amounts of these drugs may lead to coma and death; however, death is less likely with an overdose of minor tranquilizers than with an overdose of barbituates. Patients taking these should be cautioned against driving or performing tasks that require careful attention to detail and mental alertness.

Antidepressants, such as the *Tricyclic Antidepressants,* are used to elevate the patient's mood, and increase appetite and mental and physical alertness. Drugs in this group tend to take one to four weeks of use before significant changes occur in the patient's outlook. Since these drugs sometimes excite patients instead of sedating them, patients must be observed closely for reactions. These drugs include:

Elavil	Sinequan
Endep	Tofranil
Asendine	Aventyl
Morpramin	Vivactil
Adapin	Marplan
Presamine	Janimine

Common side effects include dry mouth, fatigue, weakness, nausea, increased appetite, increased perspiration, heartburn, and sensitivity to sunlight. *Serious side effects* include blurred vision, constipation, irregular heartbeat, problems urinating, headache, eye pain, fainting, hallucination, vomiting, unusually slow pulse, seizures, skin rash, sore throat and fever, and yellowing of eyes and skin.

Serious side effects include blurred vision, constipation, irregular heartbeat, problems urinating, headache, eye pain, fainting, hallucination, vomiting, unusually slow pulse, seizures, skin rash, sore throat and fever, and yellowing of eyes and skin.

Monoamineoxidose Inhibitors (MAO Inhibitors) are sometimes used for depression, but can have *very* serious side effects, and can also lead to serious hypertensive crisis. Their use must be very closely monitored. Their use with some over-the-counter drugs can be very serious. Foods containing Typtophen or Tyramine (some examples: caffeine, chocolate, herring, beans, chicken liver, cheese, beer, pickles, wine) should be avoided also. *Side effects* to watch for include severe headaches, stiff neck, nausea, vomiting, dilated pupils, and cold, clammy skin. A hypertensive crisis requires *immediate* treatment. These drugs include: Marplan, Nardil, Parnate, and Ludiomil.

In addition to the above psychotropic drugs, sedatives, hypnotics, anticonvulsants, and antiparkinsons drugs are also used. Since the exam announcement includes uses and reactions of only the psychotropic drugs, we will not review the non-psychotropic drugs. We will mention, however, the use and reactions of *Lithium Carbonate* (also known as Eskolith, Lithane,

Lithobid, and Lithonate). This drug is primarily used in the treatment of manic depressive psychoses since it is effective in decreasing excessive motor activity, talking, and unstable behavior by acting on the brain's metabolism. It also decreases swings in mood. The correct dose is close to the overdose level for this drug, so it is important to watch closely for symptoms and to report them immediately. *Common side effects* include dry mouth, metal taste, slightly increased urination, hand tremors, increased appetite, and fatigue. *Serious side effects* include greatly increased urination, nausea, vomiting, diarrhea, loss of muscle coordination, muscle cramps or weakness, irritability, confusion, slurred speech, blackout spells, and coma. These side effects require medical attention. *Special Considerations:* This drug must sometimes be taken from one to several weeks before the resident feels better. Hot weather, hot baths, and too much exercise can be dangerous, as too much perspiring can lead to an overdose. The person should drink two to three quarts of fluid a day, but should not drink large quantities of caffeine-containing beverages like coffee, tea, or colas.

GLOSSARY OF BASIC PSYCHIATRIC TERMS

TABLE OF CONTENTS

	Page
Accident Prone ... Anxiety	1
Anxiety Reaction (Anxiety Neurosis) ... Catatonic State	2
Character Disorder ... Conversion	3
Conversion Reaction ... Depression	4
Disorientation ... Environment	5
Epilepsy ... Free Association	6
Frustration ... Hypnosis (Hypnotic Trance)	7
Hypochondriasis ... Insight	8
Instinct ... Looseness of Association	9
Maladjustment ... Mind	10
Motivation ... Object	11
Obsession ... Paranoid State	12
Pathogenesis ... Projective Tests	13
Psyche ... Psychosomatic	14
Psychosurgery ... Reversal	15
Sadism ... Stress	16
Subject ... Turning Against the Self	17
Unconscious ... Waxy Flexibility	18

GLOSSARY OF BASIC PSYCHIATRIC TERMS

A

ACCIDENT PRONE
Special susceptibility to accidents due to psychological causes.

ADDICTION
A descriptive name for a type of psychiatric illness (character disorder) characterized by excessive psychological and/or physiologic dependence upon the intake of some substance, as, for example, alcohol or an opiate.

ADJUSTMENT
The series of technics or processes by which the individual strives to meet the continuous changes that take place within himself and in his environment. Synonym: adaptation. (Some authorities consider adjustment to refer particularly to psychological activity and adaptation to physiologic activity.)

AFFECT
Generalized feeling tone. (Usually considered to be more persistent than emotion and less so than mood.)

Affective, pertaining to affect.

Affective psychosis, a psychosis characterized by an extreme alteration in mood in the direction of mania or of depression.

AGGRESSION (Aggressive Drive)
A term used in various ways; in the usq.ge of psychiatry, an instinct-like force, much influenced by early experience, motivating the individual to destructive activity.

AIM
Intention or purpose; in psychiatric literature the term is used chiefly in the discussion of instincts; the *aim* of an instinctual drive may be defined as an action on the part of the individual that involves the *object* of the drive and results in gratification. Thus, the aim of the instinctual drive, hunger, is eating.

AMBIVALENCE
The experiencing of contradictory strivings or emotions toward an object or situation. In extreme form, characteristic of *schizophrenia.*

ANAL CHARACTER (PERSONALITY)
(1) In psychoanalysis a pattern of behavior in an adult that originates in the anal eroticism of infancy and is characterized by such traits as excessive orderliness, miserliness, and obstinacy.
(2) A type of character (personality) disorder in which many of the individual's conflicts and defenses remain those appropriate to the muscle-training period, usually characterized by such traits as parsimony, rigidity, and pedantry.

ANAL PERIOD
One of the developmental stages; the muscle-training period.

ANTHROPOLOGY
The science of man or mankind in the widest sense; the history of human society; the developmental aspects of man as a species.

ANXIETY
(1) Apprehension, the source of which is largely unknown or unrecognized. It is different from fear, which is the emotional response to a consciously recognized and usually external danger.
(2) A state of tension and distress akin to fear, but produced by the threatened loss of inner control rather than by an external danger.

Anxiety attack, a phenomenon characterized by intense feelings of anxiety plus such physiologic manifestations as increased pulse and respiratory rates and increased perspiration.

ANXIETY REACTION (ANXIETY NEUROSIS)

A *psychoneurosis* characterized by the more or less continuous presence of anxiety in excess of normal and occasional clear-cut *anxiety attacks.*

ATTITUDE

One's physical and emotional position and manner with respect to another person, thing, or situation.

Attitude therapy, a method of treatment utilizing the assumption by the personnel of attitudes calculated to exert a favorable effect upon the patient.

AUTISM

Self-preoccupation with loss of interest in and appreciation of other persons and socially accepted behavior. *Autistic thinking,* thought processes determined by inner needs and relatively uninfluenced by environmental considerations, a characteristic of *schizophrenia.*

AUTISTIC CHILD

In child psychiatry, a child who responds chiefly to inner thoughts who does not relate to his environment, and whose overall functioning is immature and often appears retarded.

B

BASIC DRIVE

In human psychology, one of a group of hereditarily transmitted motivating forces, deriving ultimately from biochemical changes within the organism; used synonymously with instinct.

BEHAVIOR (HUMAN)

All the activity of a human being that is capable of observation by another person.

BEHAVIOR DISORDER

See Personality Disorder.

BLOCKING

(1) Difficulty in recollection, or interruption of a train of thought or speech, caused by unconscious emotional factors.
(2) An involuntary, functional interference with a person's thinking, memory or communication. (Usually the term is employed with reference to a psychotherapeutic situation.)

C

CASTRATION

Literally, the removal or the destruction of the gonads (ovaries or testes). In psychoanalytic terminology, the loss of the penis.

CASTRATION ANXIETY

Anxiety due to danger (fantasied) of loss of the genitals or injuries to them. May be precipitated by everyday events that have symbolic significance and appear to be threatening, such as loss of job, loss of a tooth, or an experience of ricidule or humiliation.

CATALEPSY

A condition usually characterized by trance-like states. May occur in organic or psychological disorders or under hypnosis.

CATATONIC STATE (Catatonia)

(1) A state characterized by immobility with, muscular rigidity or inflexibility and at times by excitability. Virtually always a symptom of schizophrenia.
(2) One of the four classic schizophrenic subgroups (syndromes), usually beginning at a

relatively early age and characterized by a rapid onset and interference with normal motor function.

CHARACTER DISORDER
See Personality Disorder.

COMPENSATION
(1) A defense mechanism, operating unconsciously, by which the individual attempts to make up for (i.e., to compensate for) real or fancied deficiencies.
(2) A conscious process in which the individual strives to make up for real or imagined defects in such areas as physique, performance, skills, or psychological attributes.

COMPLEX
(1) A group of associated ideas that have a common emotional tie. These are largely unconscious and significantly influence attitudes and associations. Examples are:

Inferiority Complex - Feelings of inferiority stemming from real or imagined physical or social inadequacies that may cause anxiety or other adverse reactions. The individual may overcompensate by excessive ambition or by the development of special skills, often in the very field in which he was originally handicapped.

Oedipus Complex - Attachment of the child for the parent of the opposite sex, accompanied by envious and aggressive feelings toward the parent of the same sex. These feelings are largely repressed (i.e., made unconscious) because of the fear of displeasure or punishment by the parent of the same sex. In its original use, the term applied only to the male child.

(2) In psychoanalytic terminology, a group of associated ideas and feelings that, though unconscious, influence the subject's conscious attitudes and behavior.

COMPULSION
(1) An insistent, repetitive, and unwanted urge to perform an act that is contrary to the person's ordinary conscious wishes or standards. Failure to perform the compulsive act results in overt anxiety.
(2) An act that is carried out, in some degree, against the subject's conscious wishes, either to avoid the anxiety that would otherwise appear, or to dispel a disturbing *obsession*.
compulsive, pertaining to a compulsion.

COMPULSIVE PERSONALITY
A type of personality disorder; more specifically, a type of neurotic personality. *See* Anal Character (Personality).

CONFLICT
A struggle between two or more opposing forces. *Intrapersonal* (*intrapsychic*; *conflict*, a struggle between forces within a single personality. *Interpersonal conflict,* a struggle between two or more individuals.

CONGENITAL
Present from birth; mayor may not be hereditary.

CONSCIENCE
Equivalent to the conscious portion of the superego; in strict psychoanalytic terminology, the "ego ideal."

CONSCIOUS
Aware or sensible; "mentally awake."

CONVERSION
Sensory or motor dysfunctions by which the subject gives symbolic expression to a conflict (of which he is not conscious).

CONVERSION REACTION
A psychoneurosis, formerly called "conversion hysteria," characterized by conversions.

CULTURE
The characteristic attainments of a people.

CYCLOTHYMIA
A tendency or a proneness to repeated, exaggerated, largely irrational alterations in mood, usually between euphoria and depression.

Cyclothymic, pertaining to cyclothymia.

Cyclothymia personality, a type of psychotic personality disorder, often the precursor of manic-depressive psychosis.

D

DEATH INSTINCT (Thanatos)
In Freudian theory, the unconscious drive toward dissolution and death. Coexists with and is in opposition to the life instinct (Eros).

DEFENSE MECHANISM
(1) A specific process, operating unconsciously, that is employed to seek relief from emotional conflict and freedom from anxiety.
(2) A psychological technic performed by the ego but carried out below the subject's threshold of awareness, designed to ward off anxiety or unpleasant tensions.

DELIRIUM
An altered level of consciousness (awareness), often acute and in most instances reversible, manifested by disorientation and confusion and induced by an interference with the metabolic processes of the neurons of the brain. *Delirium tremens,* an agitated delirious state occurring as a complication of chronic alcoholism.

DELUSION
A fixed idea, arising out of the subject's inner needs and contrary to the observed facts as these are interpreted by normal persons under the same circumstances; a symptom of psychosis.

DEMENTIA
A chronic, typically irreversible deterioration of intellectual capacities, due to organic disease of the brain that has produced structural changes (the actual death of neurons).

Dementia paralytica, formerly "paresis," a chronic syphilitic inflammation of the brain and its membranous coverings resulting, if untreated, in progressive dementia and paralysis and ultimately in death.

Dementia praecox, an old (obsolescent) (and misleading) term for schizophrenia.

DENIAL
A *defense mechanism* in which the ego refuses to allow awareness of some aspect of reality.

DEPRESSION
(1) Psychiatrically, a morbid sadness, dejection, or melancholy; to be differentiated from grief, which is realistic and proportionate to what has been lost. A depression may be a symptom of any psychiatric disorder or may constitute its principal manifestation.
(2) A pathologic state brought on by feelings of loss and/or guilt and characterized by sadness and a lowering of self-esteem.

Neurotic depressive reaction, a state of depression of neurotic intensity in which *reality-testing* is largely unimpaired and in which physiologic disturbances, if present, are usually mild.

Psychotic depressive reaction, a state of depression of psychotic intensity in which reality-testing is severely impaired and in which physiologic disturbances *(vegetative signs)* are usually conspicuous.

Reactive depression, a state of depression -- intensity not specified -- for which the precipitating stress can be clearly discerned and seen to be of some magnitude.

DISORIENTATION

Confusion of the subject with respect to such information as the correct time and place, a knowledge of his personal identity and an understanding of his situation; typically seen in *delirium* and *dementia.*

DISPLACEMENT

A general term for a group of psychological phenomena (technics) in which certain strivings or feelings are (unconsciously) transferred from one object, activity, or situation to another (which acquires a similar meaning). The defense technic of sublimation is one example of a successful displacement.

DISSOCIATION

A breaking of psychic connections, of associations.

DISSOCIATIVE REACTION

Formerly called "hysterical amnesia." A psychoneurosis in which a group of thoughts, feelings and memories becomes separated from the rest of the personality.

DRIVE

See Basic Drive.

DYNAMIC (PSYCHODYNAMIC)

Pertaining to the forces operating within the personality and determining the behavior, particularly unconscious forces. Dynamic psychiatry, a psychiatry concerned with the understanding of such motivating forces.

E

EGO

(1) In psychoanalytic theory, one of the three major divisions of human personality, the others being the id and superego. The ego, commonly identified with consciousness of self, is the mental agent mediating among three contending forces: the external demands of social pressure or reality; the primitive instinctual demands arising from the id imbedded as it is in the deepest level of the unconscious; and the claims of the superego, born of parental and social prohibitions and functioning as an internal censor or "conscience."

(2) One of the three agencies or aspects of the mind, the ego is the aspect that is in contact with the environment through the sensory apparatus, that appriases environmental and inner changes and that directs behavior through its control of the motor apparatus.

ELECTROCONVULSIVE THERAPY (E.C.T., ELECTROSHOCK THERAPY)

A method of treatment of psychiatric disorders by passing an electric current through the brain, producing an artificial seizure.

ELECTROENCEPHALOGRAPH

An instrument, based on the string galvanometer, for measuring very small changes in potential derived from the electrical activity of the neurons of the brain. *Electroencephalogram,* the record obtained with the electroencephalograph, a "brain-wave tracing."

EMPATHY

(1) An objective awareness of the feelings, emotions, and behavior of another person. To be distinguished from sympathy, which is usually nonobjective and noncritical.

(2) A deep recognition of the significance of another person's behavior, which retains a certain objectivity and yet involves intellectual, emotional and motivational experiences corresponding to those of the other person.

ENVIRONMENT

All that surrounds the individual, including living and non-living, material and immaterial elements.

EPILEPSY

A disorder characterized by periodic seizures, and sometimes accompanied by a loss of consciousness. May be caused by organic or emotional disturbances.

Major epilepsy (grand mal) - Characterized by gross convulsive seizures, with loss of consciousness.

Minor epilepsy (petit mal) - Minor nonconvulsive epileptic seizures; may be limited to only momentary lapses of consciousness.

ETHOLOGY

The scientific study of the instincts. *Ethologist,* one who makes a scientific study of the instincts.

ETIOLOGY

Pertaining to causation; in medicine and nursing, pertaining to the causation of disease.

EUPHORIA

(1) An exaggerated feeling of physical and emotional well-being inconsonant with reality.

(2) An exaggerated (unrealistic) sense of well-being.

EXHIBITIONISM

Erotic pleasure in exposing the body to the view of others; in adults, a form of perversion when it is the principal form of erotic expression.

EXTROVERSION

A state in which attention and energies are largely directed outward from the self, as opposed to interest primarily directed toward the self, as in introversion.

F

FACULTY

A power or a function, especially a mental one.

FAMILY TRIANGLE

The situation, involving the child and the parents, in which the child experiences the wish to displace the parent of the same sex and possess the parent of the opposite sex. Family-triangle period, a developmental phase characterized by maximum intensity of these strivings. Synonymous with *Oedipal period.*

FANTASY (PHANTASY)

An image -- conscious or unconscious -- formed by recombinations of memories and interpretations of them.

FEAR

An experience, having both psychological and physiologic components, stimulated by the awareness of impending danger in the environment.

FIXATION

The persistence into later life of interests and behavior patterns appropriate to an earlier developmental phase.

FLATNESS OF AFFECT

A lack of normal emotional responsiveness, especially characteristic of *schizophrenia*.

FLIGHT OF IDEAS

A morbid type of thought sequence manifested through speech, characterized by its rapidity and by numerous and sudden shifts in topics, but that tends to be comprehensible to the normal observer. Typical of mania.

FREE ASSOCIATION

(1) In psychoanalytic therapy, spontaneous, uncensored verbalization by the patient of whatever comes to mind.

(2) A technic, used in *psychoanalysis,* in which the patient reports verbally his thoughts, emotions and sensations in whatever order they occur, making no effort at deliberate organization, censorship, or control.

FRUSTRATION

A blocking or nongratification of needs.

FUGUE

A major state of personality dissociation characterized by amnesia and actual physical flight from the immediate environment.

FUNCTIONAL

Pertaining solely or primarily to function. *Functional psychosis,* a psychosis occurring on the basis of disturbed mental functioning in the absence of structural brain damage.

G

GARRULOUSNESS

Excessive talkativeness, especially about trivial things.

GENITAL PHASE (OF DEVELOPMENT)

In psychoanalytic terminology, a synonym for emotional maturity.

GROUP

Any two or more persons who are set off from others, either temporarily or permanently, by a special type of association (relationship), as, for example, an important common interest.

Group therapy, a form of *psychotherapy* taking place among a group of patients under the guidance of a therapist.

H

HALLUCINATION

A sensory experience, occurring (in the absence of adequate reality-testing) on the basis of the subject's inner needs and independently of stimulation from the environment.

HALLUCINOGEN

A chemical substance capable of inducing hallucinations.

HEBEPHRENIA

One of the classic schizophrenic subgroups, the one having the most ominous prognosis. *Hebephrenic schizophrenia* is a synonym.

HEREDITARY

Genetically transmitted from parent to offspring.

HETEROSEXUAL

Pertaining to the opposite sex.

HOMEOSTASIS

A tendency to uniformity and stability in the normal body states of the organism (Walter B. Cannon).

HOMOSEXUAL

(adj.) Pertaining to an erotic interest in members of one's own sex. (noun) One having an erotic interest in members of his own sex.

(1) Sexual attraction or relationship between members of the same sex.

Latent homosexuality - A condition characterized by unconscious homosexual desires.

Overt homosexuality - Homosexuality that is consciously recognized or practiced.

(2) *Homosexuality,* a condition characterized by the subject's having an erotic interest in members of his own sex, a form of *personality disorder.*

HYPNOSIS (HYPNOTIC TRANCE)

(1) A state of increased receptivity to suggestion and direction, initially induced by the

influence of another person. The degree may vary from mild suggestibility to a trance state so profound as to be used in surgical operations.

(2) An artificially induced state, akin to sleep, in which the subject enters into so close a relationship with the hypnotist that the suggestions of the latter become virtually indistinguishable from the activity of his own ego.

HYPOCHONDRIASIS

(1) Overconcern with the state of physical or emotional health, accompanied by various bodily complaints without demonstrable organic pathology.

(2) A severe type of *psychoneurosis,* characterized by a morbid preoccupation with one's body and a partial withdrawal of interest from the environment. *Hypochondriac,* one afflicted with hypochondriasis.

HYSTERIA

A *psychoneurosis;* the older term for the conditions now designated as *conversion reaction* and *dissociative reaction.*

HYSTERICAL PERSONALITY

(1) A personality type characterized by shifting emotional feelings, susceptibility to suggestion, impulsive behavior, attention seeking, immaturity, and self-absorption; not necessarily disabling.

(2) A form of *personality disorder (neurotic personality)* characterized by conflicts and defenses similar to those found in persons with hysteria.
Hysteric, one afflicted with hysteria.

I

ID

The one of the three agencies or aspects of the mind that contains the psychic representations of the instinctual drives.

IDEATION

The process of forming ideas.

IDENTIFICATION

The adoption -- unconsciously -- of some of the characteristics of another person. Strictly speaking, the term refers to the result of the defense mechanism of *introjection.* (Sometimes identification and introjection are used loosely as synonyms.)

ILLUSION

A false perceptual experience occurring in response to an environmental stimulus; usually a symptom of serious mental illness.

INCEST

Culturally prohibited sexual relations between members of a family, usually persons closely related by blood, as father and daughter, mother and son, or brother and sister. INHIBITION

(1) Interference with or restriction of activities; the result of an unconscious defense against forbidden instinctual drives.

(2) The restraining or the stopping of a process; in psychiatry, the term usually refers to an inner force that opposes the gratification of a basic drive.

INSANITY

Now a term of legal or medicolegal significance only, referring to a mental disorder of sufficient gravity to bring the subject under special legal restrictions and immunities.

INSIGHT

(1) Self-understanding. A major goal of psychotherapy. The extent of the individual's understanding of the origin, nature, and mechanisms of his attitudes and behavior.

(2) In the broad psychiatric sense, the patient's knowledge that he suffers from an emo-

tional illness; in the narrow psychiatric sense, the patient's knowledge of the specific, hitherto unconscious, meaning of his symptom(s) or of some other aspect of illness.

INSTINCT

A term of many meanings; in dynamic psychiatric usage it is usually considered as synonymous with *basic drive*.

INSULIN COMA THERAPY

A method of treatment of psychoses through the induction of a series of comas by means of insulin injections.

INTERNALIZE

To place within (the mind). Said of a conflict or a state of tension that, in its original form, existed between an individual and some aspect of his environment, but that has come to exist within the mind (i.e., between one aspect of the personality and another). Thus *anxiety* is often found to be an *internalized fear*.

INTERPERSONAL

Existing between two or more individuals; often contrasted with intrapersonal.

INTERPRETATION

A scientific guess, made by a psychotherapist about a patient, explaining some aspect of the latter's thoughts, feelings or behavior.

INTRAPERSONAL (INTRAPSYCHIC)

Existing within a mind or a personality; often contrasted with *interpersonal*.

INTROJECTION

One of the *defense mechanisms;* the psychological process whereby a quality or an attribute of another person is taken into and made a part of the subject's personality (unconsciously). Often used loosely as synonymous with *identification*.

INVOLUTION (INVOLUTIONAL PERIOD)

A period in late middle age in which retrogressive physiologic changes take place, causing a loss of the capacity for reproduction. *Involutional psychosis,* a psychosis for which a major precipitating factor has been the advent of involution.

ISOLATION

One of the *defense mechanisms;* the psychological process whereby the actual facts of an experience are allowed to remain in consciousness, but the linkage between these facts and the related emotions or impulses is broken.

L

LATENCY (LATENCY PERIOD)

One of the phases of human development, occurring between the *family-triangle period* and *puberty* (approximately, ages 6 to 11 or 12 years), characterized by a relative instinctual quiescence coupled with a rapid intellectual development.

LEVELS OF AWARENESS (LEVELS OF CONSCIOUSNESS)

An expression referring to the fact that mental activity takes place with varying degrees of the subject's awareness: an individual may be entirely unaware, dimly aware, or fully aware of a given bit of mental activity.

LIBIDO

An inclusive term for the sexual-social drives.

LOBOTOMY (PREFRONTAL)

A psychosurgical procedure in which certain tracts of the brain are severed, thus stopping the interaction between the prefrontal areas (of the cerebral cortex) and the rest of the brain. Sometimes used as a therapeutic measure in severe psychoses.

LOOSENESS OF ASSOCIATION

A symptom of serious mental illness, usually of *schizophrenia,* in which the logical connections between a patient's successive thoughts are absent or are not discernible to the observer.

M

MALADJUSTMENT

A state of disequilibrium between the individual and his environment, in which his needs are not being gratified.

MALINGER

To feign an illness.

Malingerer, one who feigns an illness.

MANIA

(1) A suffix denoting a pathological preoccupation with some desire, idea, or activity; a morbid compulsion. Some frequently encountered manias are: *dipsomania,* compulsion to drink alcoholic beverages; *egomania,* pathological preoccupation with self; *kleptomania,* compulsion to steal; *megalomania,* pathological preoccupation with delusions of power or wealth; *monomania,* pathological preoccupation with one subject; *necromania,* pathological preoccupation with the dead; pyromania, morbid compulsion to set fires.

(2) A morbid state of extreme euphoria and excitement with loss of reality-testing; one of the phases of *manic-depressive psychosis.*

Manic (adj.), pertaining to mania; (noun), one who suffers from mania.

MANIC-DEPRESSIVE REACTION

A group of psychiatric disorders marked by conspicuous mood swings, ranging from normal to elation or to depression, or alternating. Officially regarded as a psychosis but may also exist in milder form.

Depressed phase - Characterized by depression of mood with retardation and inhibition of thinking and physical activity.

Manic phase - Characterized by depression of mood with retardation of thought, speech, and bodily motion, and by elation or grandiosity of mood, and irritability.

MASOCHISM

(1) Pleasure derived from undergoing physical or psychological pain inflicted by oneself or by others. It may be consciously sought or unconsciously arranged or invited. Present to some degree in all human relations and to greater degrees in all psychiatric disorders. It is the converse of sadism, in which pain is inflicted on another, and the two tend to coexist in the same individual.

(2) Finding gratification in pain; in the narrow sense, one of the perversions.

MASTURBATION

Erotic stimulation of one's external genitalia.

MATURITY

The state of being fully adult; psychologically characterized particularly by the ability to love others in a relatively non-selfish way.

MECHANISM (MENTAL, DEFENSE)

See Defense Mechanism.

MILIEU

The total environment, emotional as well as physical.

Milieu therapy, treatment by means of controlled modifications of the patient's environment.

MIND

The body in action as a unit. *Mental,* pertaining to mind as thus defined. *Mental illness,* accurately speaking, any illness of the mind, regardless of severity; often incorrectly restricted to severe psychiatric conditions.

MOTIVATION
A psychological state that incites to action.

MOURNING
The process that follows upon the loss of a love object, through which the subject gradually frees himself from the disequilibrium caused by the loss.

MULTIPLE PERSONALITY
A morbid condition, related to *dissociative reaction,* in which the normal organization of the personality is split up into distinct portions, all having a fairly complex organization of their own. (If there are only two such portions, the term dual personality is used.)

MUSCLE-TRAINING PERIOD
One of the developmental stages, lasting from the end of *infancy* to the beginning of the *family-triangle period* (about age 1½ to age 3), during which the child receives training in sphincter control and other motor activities. Synonymous with *anal period.*

MYELIN
The fatlike substance that forms a sheath around the medullated nerve fibers. *Myelinization,* the process of acquiring a myelin sheath.

N

NARCISSISM (NARCISM)
(1) Self-love, as opposed to object-love (love of another person). Some degree of narcissism is considered healthy and normal, but an excess interferes with relations with others.
(2) Self-love; extreme narcissism is the emotional position found in the newborn infant and in certain psychoses. The term is derived from the Greek legend of Narcissus, a youth who fell in love with his own image.

Narcissistic, loving oneself excessively in a childish or an infantile fashion.

NARCOSYNTHESIS
A form of psychiatric treatment in which contact is established with the patient while he is under the influence of a hypnotic drug.

NEGATIVISM
A tendency to resist suggestions or requests, often accompanied by a response that is, in some sense, the opposite of the one sought. *Negativistic,* expressing negativism.

NEOLOGISM
A newly coined word, or the act of coining such a word; a phenomenon seen in *schizophrenia* and in some cases of *organic brain disease.*

NEURASTHENIA
One of the psychoneuroses, related to *anxiety reaction,* characterized by chronic feelings of fatigue and tension and often by disturbances in the sexual function and minor disturbances in the digestive function.

NEUROPHYSIOLOGY
The physiology of the nervous sytem. *Neurophysiologist,* a specialist in neurophysiology.

NEUROSIS
See psychoneurosis.

O

OBJECT
A term with several meanings. In the broadest sense, it is used in contrast with the term *subject* and means anything in the environment, including another person. In a narrower sense, *object* refers to "a satisfying something" in the environment that is capable of offering instinctual gratification. Thus, *love object* refers to a person toward whom the subject experiences libidinal strivings.

OBSESSION
(1) Persistent, unwanted idea or impulse that cannot be eliminated by logic or reasoning.
(2) A thought, recognized by the subject as more or less irrational, that persistently recurs, despite the subject's conscious wish to avoid or ignore it.
obsessive, pertaining to or afflicted with obsessions.

OBSESSIVE-COMPULSIVE NEUROSIS
One of the psychoneuroses, characterized by *obsessions* and *compulsions* and an underlying personality type whose conflicts involve problems of the muscle-training period.

OEDIPUS
A character in Greek legend, who unwittingly killed his father and married his mother and was subsequently punished by the gods by being blinded. *Oedipus complex,* a term referring to the erotic attachment of the (normal as well as neurotic) small child to the parent of the opposite sex, repressed largely because of the fear of bodily mutilation ("castration") by the presumedly jealous parent of the same sex. *Oedipal period,* same as *family-triangle period.*

ORAL PERIOD
The first postuterine developmental period, roughly synonymous with infancy, in which the individual's central experiences are those involved in the act of sucking.

ORAL PERSONALITY
One of the *personality disorders,* characterized by the persistence in adult life of problems and defenses appropriate to the *oral period* of development.

ORGANIC
Based on structural alterations, gross or microscopic. *Organic psychosis,* a psychosis the etiology of which involves structural damage. (The term also includes *toxic psychosis,* in which the physical alterations are at a submicroscopic -- i.e., chemical -- level.)

ORGANISM
A general term for any living creature, including man.

OVERCOMPENSATION
A conscious or unconscious process in which a real or fancied physical or psychological deficit inspires exaggerated correction.

OVERT
Discernible; "out in the open."

P

PANIC (PANIC REACTION)
A morbid state characterized by extreme fear and/or anxiety, causing a temporary disorganization of the personality.

PARANOIA
Traditionally considered to be one of the three major functional (nonorganic) psychoses, but now generally thought to be one variety of paranoid schizophrenia. A pathologic state, characterized by extreme suspiciousness and highly organized delusions of persecution, occurring in the presence of a clear sensorium and relatively appropriate affective responses.

Paranoid, pertaining to paranoia or paranoid schizophrenia.

Paranoid reaction, an acute, often self-limited state, resembling paranoia; the term is inclusive of paranoid syndromes arising on the basis of organic disease.

PARANOID SCHIZOPHRENIA
One of the four major schizophrenic subgroups, characterized by the usual features of *schizophrenia* plus delusions of persecution and/or grandeur (often loosely organized), auditory hallucinations in keeping with the delusions, and a marked, generalized suspiciousness.

PARANOID STATE
Characterized by delusions of persecution. A paranoid state may be of short duration or

PATHOGENESIS

The mode of development of disease states.

PERCEPTION

A psychological experience in which sensory stimuli are integrated to form an image (the significance of which is influenced by past experiences).

PERSONALITY

The whole group of adjustment technics and equipment that are characteristic for a given individual in meeting the various situations of life.

PERSONALITY DISORDER

In the limited (diagnostic) sense, a type of psychiatric illness in which the patient's inner difficulties are revealed, not by specific symptoms but by an unhealthy pattern of living. Thus used, roughly synonymous with *character disorder* and *behavior disorder*. In a broader sense, "disorder of the personality" is often used as equivalent to "mental illness" or "emotional illness:'

PERVERSION (SEXUAL PERVERSION)

A form of personality disorder, characterized by an alteration from the normal of the *aim* and/or the *object* of libidinal strivings. Examples: *sadism, masochism, voyeurism.*

PHANTASY

See fantasy.

PHOBIA

(1) An obsessive, unrealistic fear of an external object or situation. Some of the common phobias are *acrophobia,* fear of heights; *agoraphobia,* fear of open places; claustrophobia, fear of closed spaces; *mysophobia,* fear of dirt and germs; *xenophobia, fear* of *strangers.*

(2) The dread of an object, an act or a situation that is not realistically dangerous, but that has come to represent a danger.

Phobic, pertaining to phobias.

PHOBIC REACTION

One of the psychoneuroses, formerly called *anxiety hysteria,* characterized by the presence of phobias.

PRECONSCIOUS

One of the three levels of *awareness,* the quality attaching to an idea, a sensation or an emotion of which the subject is not spontaneously aware but can become aware with effort.

PREMORBID PERSONALITY

The status of an individual's personality (conflicts, defenses, strengths, weaknesses) before the onset of clinical illness.

PRIMARY GAIN

The adjustment (adaptational) value of a neurotic symptom per se.

PROJECTION

One of the *defense mechanisms,* a technic whereby feelings, wishes or attitudes, originating within the subject, are attributed by him to persons or other objects in his environment.

PROJECTIVE TESTS

(1) Psychological tests used as a diagnostic tool. Among the most common projective tests is the Rorschach (inkblot) test.

(2) A relatively unstructured, although standardized, psychological test in which the subject is called upon to respond with a minimum of intellectual restrictions, thereby revealing characteristic drives, defenses and attitudes. (Examples are the Rorschach and the Thematic Apperception Tests.)

PSYCHE
Actually synonymous with *mind;* frequently used in expressions suggesting a mind-body duality, as, for example, "psychosomatic," "psychophysiologic," and "psychic versus organic factors:'

PSYCHIATRY
That branch of medicine that deals with the causes, the diagnosis, the treatment and the prevention of mental disorders.

Psychiatrist, a physician specializing in psychiatry.

Psychiatric nurse, a nurse specializing in the care of patients having mental disorders.

Psychiatric team, a group of professional and semiprofessional persons working together under the direction of a psychiatrist in the treatment of psychiatric, patients. (Usually the membership of such a team includes psychiatrist, psychiatric nurse, clinical psychologist, psychiatric social worker, occupational therapist, and psychiatric aide.)

PSYCHOANALYSIS
(1) A theory of human development and behavior, a method of research, and a system of psychotherapy, originally described by Sigmund Freud (1856-1939). Through analysis of free associations and interpretation of dreams, emotions and behavior are traced to the influence of repressed instinctual drives in the unconscious. Psychoanalytic treatment seeks to eliminate or diminish the undesirable effects of unconscious conflicts by making the patient aware of their existence, origin, and inappropriate expression.

(2) The term designates 1. a *method* of (a) psychotherapy and (b) psychological research, and 2. a body of *facts and theories* of human psychology. Both the method and the body of knowledge represent the work of Sigmund Freud and his followers. *Psychoanalyst,* a professional person, usually a physician, who has received specialized formal training in the theory and the practice of psychoanalysis.

PSYCHONEUROSIS (NEUROSIS)
(1) One of the two major categories of emotional illness, the other being the psychoses. It is usually less severe than a psychosis, with minimal loss of contact with reality.

(2) A mild to moderately severe illness of the personality (mind), in which the ego function of reality-testing is not gravely impaired, and in which the maladjustment to life is of a relatively limited nature.

Psychoneurotic, pertaining to or characteristic of a psychoneurosis.

PSYCHOPATHIC PERSONALITY
An older term for one of the varieties of *personality disorder,* roughly synonymous with the current (official) category of "sociopathic personality disturbance," a form of illness characterized by emotional immaturity, the use of short-term values and behavior that is asocial or antisocial.

PSYCHOSIS
(1) A major mental disorder of organic and/or emotional origin in which there is a departure from normal patterns of thinking, feeling, and acting. Commonly characterized by loss of contact with reality, distortion of perception, regressive behavior and attitudes, diminished control of elementary impulses and desires, and delusions and hallucinations. Chronic and generalized personality deterioration may occur. A majority of patients in public mental hospitals are psychotic.

(2) A very serious illness of the personality (mind), involving a major impairment of ego function, particularly with respect to reality-testing, and revealed by signs of a grave maladjustment to life.

Psychotic, pertaining to or afflicted with psychosis.

PSYCHOSOMATIC
Adjective to denote the constant and inseparable interdependence of the psyche (mind) and

the soma (body). Most commonly used to refer to illnesses in which the manifestations are primarily physical with at least a partial emotional cause.

PSYCHOSURGERY

A form of neurosurgery in which specific tracts or other limited portions of the brain are severed or destroyed with the intention of producing favorable effects upon the patient's psychological status.

PSYCHOTHERAPY

(1) The term for any type of mental treatment that is based primarily upon verbal or nonverbal communication with the patient in distinction to the use of drugs, surgery, or physical measures such as electric or insulin shock.

(2) A term with many shades of meaning. In the broadest sense it is equivalent to "psychological treatment measures;" in a narrower sense *psychotherapy* refers to a direct relationship between one or more patients and a professional person, the therapist, in which the latter endeavors "to provide new life experiences which can influence the patient in the direction of health" (Levine).

PSYCHOTIC PERSONALITY

A variety of personality disorder, synonymous with the current official term "personality pattern disturbance," in which, despite the absence of the usual clinical symptoms of psychosis, the individual's fundamental conflicts and defenses are those of a *psychotic*.

R

RATIONALIZATION

The process of constructing plausible reasons for one's responses (usually to avoid awareness of neurotic motives).

REACTION FORMATION

One of the *defense mechanisms,* a technic whereby an original attitude or set of feelings is replaced in consciousness by the opposite attitude or feelings.

REALITY-TESTING

The process of determining objective (usually external) reality, a function of the ego.

RECONSTITUTE

To form again. The term is used of a personality that, having become more or less disorganized through illness, resumes its previous defense measures and type of adjustment.

REGRESSION

(1) The partial or symbolic return to more infantile patterns of reacting.

(2) One of the *defense mechanisms;* a process in which the personality retraces developmental steps, moving backward to earlier interests, defenses, and modes of gratification.

REPRESSION

(1) A defense mechanisms, operating unconsciously, that banishes unacceptable ideas, emotions, or impulses from consciousness or that keeps out of consciousness what has never been conscious.

(2) One of the *defense mechanisms,* a technic whereby thoughts, emotions and/or sensations are thrust out of consciousness.

REVERSAL

One of the *defense mechanisms,* a technic whereby an instinctual impulse is seemingly turned into its opposite, as, for example, when *sadism* is replaced by *masochism.*

S

SADISM

A form of perversion characterized by the experiencing of erotic pleasure in inflicting pain on another person. Often used more broadly as meaning the enjoyment of cruelty. *(See Masochism.)*

SCHIZOID

Schizophrenic-like. *Schizoid personality,* a form of *personality disorder* (subgroup of *psychotic personality*) characterized by withdrawn, self-centered, often eccentric behavior.

SCHIZOPHRENIA

(1) A severe emotional disorder of psychotic depth, characteristically marked by a retreat from reality with delusion formation, hallucinations, emotional disharmony, and regressive behavior. Formerly called dementia praecox. Its prognosis has improved in recent years.

(2) One of the major *functional psychoses;* more accurately, a group of interrelated symptom syndromes, having in common a number of features, including *associative looseness, autistic thinking, ambivalence* and inappropriateness of *affect*. The classic subgroups are: *catatonic, paranoid, simple* and *hebephrenic* schizophrenia; other varieties are: *schizoaffective, undifferentiated, childhood* and *latent* schizophrenia. *Schizophrenic,* pertaining to or afflicted with schizophrenia.

SECONDARY GAIN

The adjustment value or gratification that occurs as a result of the way in which a patient's environment responds to his illness (not an integral part of the symptoms per se).

SELF-CONCEPT

A person's image of himself, usually his conscious image.

SENILE

Pertaining to (extreme) old age, particularly to the deterioration in adjustment capacity occurring in old age.

Senile psychosis, an organic psychosis resulting from the brain damage accompanying advanced age.

SHOCK TREATMENT

A form of psychiatric treatment in which electric current, insulin, or carbon dioxide is administered to the patient and results in a convulsive reaction to alter favorably the course of mental illness.

SIMPLE SCHIZOPHRENIA

One of the four classic *schizophrenia* subgroups, characterized by slow, insidious onset and chronic course, with the illness being shown by emotional coldness, withdrawal and eccentricity, rather than by more striking symptoms.

SOMATOPSYCHIC

A term of recent coinage, intended to indicate psychological effects of somatic pathology.

SPLIT PERSONALITY

A term calling attention to the schizophrenic's inappropriate-ness of affect; the "split" is thus between emotions and ideation.

STRESS

Any circumstance that taxes the adjustment capacity of the individual.

SUBJECT

The person under discussion or study, as, for example, a patient or a person upon whom an experiment is performed.

SUBLIMATION

(1) A defense mechanism, operating unconsciously, by which instinctual but consciously unacceptable drives are diverted into personally and socially acceptable channels.

(2) One of the *defense mechanisms,* the only one that is never pathogenic; a technic whereby the original aim or *object* of a basic drive is altered in a manner that allows the release of tension and, at the same time, is socially acceptable.

SUPEREGO

One of the three major aspects or agencies of the mind; similar to the term "conscience" but more inclusive since it involves both conscious and unconscious components. (*See* Ego.)

SUPPRESSION

A technic of adjustment -- differing from the *defense mechanisms* in that it is fully conscious and very rarely pathogenic -- whereby the ego denies expression to a thought or an impulse. (It is often contrasted with *repression,* which is automatic, unconsciously effected and frequently pathogenic.)

SYMBOLISM

The use of one mental image to represent another.

T

TOXIC

Pertaining to, or due to the action of, a poison.

Toxic *psychosis,* a psychosis brought about by the action of a poisonous substance or, more broadly, a psychosis brought about by any chemical interference with normal metabolic processes (grouped with the *organic psychoses*).

TRANSFERENCE

The attributing by the subject, to a figure in his current environment, of characteristics first encountered in some figure of his early life, and the experiencing of desires, fears, and other attitudes toward the current figure that originated in the relationship with the past figure. The term is most commonly used with respect to feelings of a patient toward his therapist.

Counter-transference, transference feelings of a therapist toward his patient.

TRAUMA

Harm or injury; sometimes, the circumstances productive of harm or injury. In psychiatry, the term is inclusive of purely emotional as well as physical injury.

Traumatic, harmful, pertaining to trauma.

TRAUMATIC NEUROSIS (WAR NEUROSIS)

An acute morbid reaction related to *psychoneurosis* but occurring only in response to overwhelming trauma or stress. The condition is characterized by a temporary, partial disorganization of the personality, followed by such symptoms as anxiety, restlessness, irritability, impaired concentration, evidence of autonomic dysfunction and repetitive nightmares in which the traumatic experience is "relived."

TURNING AGAINST THE SELF

One of the *defense mechanisms,* a technic in which an unacceptable drive (usually aggressive) is diverted from its original object and (unconsciously) made to operate against the self, in whole or in part.

U

UNCONSCIOUS
(1) That part of the mind the content of which is only rarely subject to awareness. It is the repository for knowledge that has never been conscious or that may have been conscious briefly and was then repressed.
(2) In psychiatry, one of the three *levels* of *awareness;* thoughts, sensations, and emotions at this level cannot enter the subject's awareness through any voluntary effort on his part, but they continue to exert effects upon his behavior.

UNDOING
One of the *defense mechanisms,* a technic in which a specific action is performed that is (unconsciously) considered by the subject to be in some sense the opposite of a previous unacceptable action (or wish), and thus to neutralize ("undo") the original action.

V

VEGETATIVE SIGNS (OF DEPRESSION)
A traditionally grouped set of findings, including anorexia, weight loss, constipation, amenorrhea, insomnia and "morning-evening variation in mood," that, when found in combination, are indicative of severe depression.

VOYEURISM
A form of *personality disorder* (more specifically, of *perversion*), in which the subject receives his principal erotic gratification in clandestine peeping.

W

WAXY FLEXIBILITY
A phenomenon, associated with *catatonic schizophrenia,* in which the body, particularly the extremities, will remain for long periods of time in any positions selected by the examiner.

www.ingramcontent.com/pod-product-compliance
Lightning Source LLC
Chambersburg PA
CBHW081825300426
44116CB00014B/2490